INSIGHT COMPACT GUIDES

NORTH YORK MOORS

Compact Guide: North York Moors is the perfect quick-reference guide to this infinitely varied destination. It tells you all you need to know about the Moors' attractions, from picturesque market towns and villages to magnificent abbeys and country houses, from endless vistas of heather to intimate coastal hideaways.

This is one of more than 70 titles in *Apa Publications'* new series of pocket-sized, easy-to-use guidebooks intended for the independent-minded traveller. *Compact Guides* are in essence travel encyclopedias in miniature, designed to be comprehensive yet portable, as well as up-to-date and authoritative.

Star Attractions

An instant reference
to some of the
North York Moors'
top attractions to
help you on
your way.

Helmsley p20

Rievaulx Abbey p22

Hutton-le-Hole p24

Lastingham p28

Hole of Horcum p33

Moors Railway p35

Mount Grace Priory p42

Whitby p46

Castle Howard p30

Staithes p55

Robin Hood's Bay p56

NORTH YORK MOORS

Introduction

Places

Culture

Leisure

Practical Information

North York Moors – A Place Apart

Opposite: the endless Moors

The North York Moors are a place apart. The most sharply defined of Britain's 11 national parks, they are bounded on two sides by steeply plunging escarpments and on a third by towering cliffs that defy the North Sea. Only where neighbouring farmland slopes up gradually from the Vale of Pickering do the Moors lack an obvious frontier. And there, outflowing rivers, slicing through the gently tilted plateaux, have carved a series of bold headlands. Like a row of lions couchant, these keep watch over the higher central moors.

The Hole of Horcum above the Vale of Pickering

Location and landscape

The Moors thus form a compact yet massive cornerstone of Yorkshire – literally north, or rather northeast, of York. Within their 553sq miles (1,380sq km) they embrace the largest unbroken expanse of heather moor in England and Wales. In late summer the heather flings a cape of regal purple across the full 40-mile (60-km) width of the Moors, from the Vale of York to the sea. Covering some 160sq miles (415sq km), it is a breathtaking sight.

Other seasons bring other colours to the moors. In spring the bright green flush of young bilberry, intimate companion of the heather, brings fresh cheer. In autumn there is mellowness in the russet tints of the bracken. And in winter the pale sun gilds a landscape of subdued greys and browns.

5

Close to nature

The Moors are arguably at their atmospheric in winter. The low sunlight exposes the bones of the landscape, the silence is often profound, and after a sudden, fierce sunset, the skyline suggests an infinity of moor. There then emerges that sense of things elemental, putting puny man in his place, that inspired Thomas Hardy's powerful description of Egdon Heath. As much as that imperial purple cloak of heather, this is the majesty of the Moors.

But while it is the sweeping expanses of heather that give the region its special identity, green fields are never far away. A network of dales, enfolding villages and farmhouses built mainly of warm, honey-coloured sandstone, penetrates the great dome of moorland. Smaller than the valleys of the Yorkshire Dales, each of these nevertheless has its own flavour: Eskdale, broader than most, gathering a string of tributary dales as threads its way to the sea at Whitby; Farndale, a springtime joy with its wild daffodils spread for seven miles along the banks of the river Dove; and Rosedale, although visibly scarred by industry, beautiful yet.

From these dales and others, little unfenced roads, with verges cropped by the hardy moor-

land sheep, twist up to reach, and run along, the ridges that divide the valleys. Somewhere nearby will be one or more of the pill-box Bronze Age burial mounds – howes – that crown most moors. And there might well be a lonely moorland cross, a feature so characteristic of the region that the best known, Young Ralph on Blakey Ridge, between Castleton and Hutton-le-Hole, has been adopted as the national park's emblem.

The views all around will be high, wide, and exhilarating. This is the essence of these moors – a liberating feeling of space. Aelred, third abbot of Rievaulx Abbey, most beautiful of several monastic ruins in the national park, captured the mood exactly in the 12th century: 'Everywhere peace, everywhere serenity, and a marvellous freedom from the tumult of the world.'

Rievaulx Abbey's setting, amid hanging woods and placid pastures deep in the Rye Valley, doesn't readily fit the concept of 'moors'. But the North York Moors national park contains a huge diversity of scenery. Even the hills vary in character.

Rising dramatically from the Cleveland Plain, the rugged Cleveland Hills contain the highest ground in the park and are the most stirring to explore. Gentler are the limestone Hambleton Hills, girdled with woods, a rampart along the Vale of York. And dissecting those 'headland hills' along the south, officially named The Tabular Hills, are narrow, steep-sided valleys, rich in wild flowers.

Then there is the coast. Soaring to 700ft (210m) at Boulby, which is the highest point on England's eastern seaboard, and second highest round the entire English coast, the cliffs run almost continuously for 36 miles (58km) between Saltburn and Scarborough. The occasional slight break in the cliffs allows just enough space for a village, with picturesque Staithes, Runswick Bay and Robin Hood's Bay tucked away out of sight from the main road. Once again, each is different: Staithes, tough and no nonsense; Runswick, the pretty one, basking by a bay that can, and frequently does, look Mediterranean; and Robin Hood's Bay – all charm and enchantment, a Lilliputian world of little lanes and sunlit squares.

Renowned worldwide is the townscape of Whitby, that matchless jumble of pantiled cottages clinging to the precipitous harbourside. The barrier of the once-hostile moors at the town's back engendered a saying that 'the only way into and out of Whitby is the sea'. When the first stagecoach ran, travellers made their wills. Captain Cook learned his seamanship on Whitby ships, which he chose for his great voyages of discovery. And Whitby lifeboat station has earned more gold medals than any other in Britain – testament to both the courage of the lifeboatmen and the treachery of the North Yorkshire coast.

6

Rievaulx Abbey

'Boats in Whitby Upper Harbour'
by Frank Sutcliffe

Man's Influence

Late summer in Bilsdale

The apparent wilderness of the moors is a delusion, however, because the landscape is almost entirely man made. After the Ice Age a dense forest sprang up. But this was gradually cleared for hunting, agriculture, fuel, and building. As nutrients leached from the ever-more impoverished soil, the acid-loving heather, which arrived soon after the ice melted around 10,000 years ago, took over.

By the early Middle Ages the moorland landscape was emerging. What secured its dominance were the vast monastic sheep runs. Inaugurated by Rievaulx, which had a breeding flock of 14,000 ewes, these prevented the remnants of the post-glacial forest from renewing themselves. The heather moors are thus the degraded product of prolonged misuse by man – a classic ecological disaster.

7

An early forester
Roseberry Topping

Industry, too, has had its ruthless way with this now prized landscape. The bent prow of Roseberry Topping, the region's most distinctive hill, is the outcome of quarrying. More marks were left on the landscape by the mining of coal, ironstone and jet – a fossilised wood made fashionable as jewellery when Queen Victoria adopted black following the death of Prince Albert. In most cases nature has healed these wounds, but the bald headland of Sandsend Ness, near Whitby, and the arid slopes of Carlton Bank, on the Cleveland Hills, still bear witness to the extraction and processing of alum shale. Regarded as Britain's first chemical industry, the alum yielded crystals used to fix colours in tanning and dyeing. Involving the use of human urine, which was collected locally, the noxious production method is explained at conserved remains of an alum works near Ravenscar.

In 1861 a standard gauge railway was thrust across the roof of the moors to fetch iron ore from Rosedale. Scaling the Cleveland escarpment by the spectacular 1 in 3 Ingleby Incline, this is now a superb walkers' highway. In Rosedale itself, huge kilns, with masonry that wouldn't disgrace the Pyramids, take their place with the region's numerous abbeys and castles in graphically evoking an epoch in the region's many-sided history.

Economy and industry

The mineral riches of the Moors are still being tapped. Approved in the teeth of fierce opposition in 1969, Britain's only potash mine operates at Boulby, where its 3,750-ft (1,140-m) shaft is the deepest in Europe. Limestone is quarried at Spaunton, near Kirkbymoorside.

But the economy rests chiefly on an inter-dependent combination of farming, tourism and grouse shooting. Though grouse shoots directly employ only a handful of people, the three-month shooting season provides much casual labour and custom for hotels. Together with sheep farming it also underpins tourism in the national park, which attracts about 11 million visitors a year. For without the maintenance of the moors for grouse, the celebrated vistas would soon look ragged and unkempt. Rotational burning creates a mosaic that provides the grouse with young heather, on whose shoots they feed, mature heather for nest sites, and older heather for shelter.

The heather's vigour is also helped by the grazing sheep. Sometimes dubbed 'the national-park keepers', the sheep also check the spread of bracken, prevent an invasion of scrub, and keep that roadside turf in pristine condition. Not least, they add life and interest to the moors. Today's 140 or so moor flocks contain about the same number of sheep, 60,000, as those of monastic times. Sheep far outnumber the human population of about 25,000.

Wildlife

Among the region's wildlife, the red grouse, target of the shooters, must hold pride of place. The only bird exclusive to Britain, it is also the only bird – in the North York Moors anyway – that remains on the open moor in winter. Its coarse yet cheerful call, uttered as it flies over the heather and often written as 'go-back go-back go-back', is the archetypal sound of the North York Moors.

In spring the grouse is joined by other moor birds, notably snipe, plover and golden plover. The Moors are also home to England's largest, though modest, population of merlins. The Swainby moors are one of the strongholds of this small, darting hawk. Also seen on occasion is the hen harrier, a truly magnificent bird with enormous wing span, that hunts by flying low over the heather and suddenly swooping sideways.

About 20 percent of the moors is forested – another element in its diversity. The once dark, regimented and largely lifeless forests are being subtly 'restructured' to

Checking the spread of bracken

8

Out shooting
The one that got away

look better and sustain more wildlife. Among birds they have already attracted are pine-seed-eating crossbills and siskins, a kind of finch. And in their insect-rich young plantations, the nightjar has staged a major comeback. Organised walks to nightjar nesting sites give visitors the chance to hear the male's peculiar 'churring' call, likened to the throbbing of a two stroke engine, and perhaps glimpse the birds hurtling after insects. The forests have also boosted the population of roe deer. These are now commonly seen throughout the national park, which also supports smaller numbers of red and fallow deer.

Waterfowl

Several species of flower reach their northern or southern limit in the moors. Among the latter, on Levisham Moor, are two arctic-alpine species – chickweed wintergreen and dwarf cornel, a kind of miniature dogwood. In Kirkdale, one of those steep Tabular Hills' valleys, the rare May Lily blossoms on its only native site in Britain. But while other uncommon species, like globeflower and bird's eye primrose, are also found, it is perhaps the more familiar flowers that give most delight. The Farndale daffodils, of course, but also carpets of bluebells – at Oldstead, Glaisdale, Hasty Bank, near Stokesley, and other places. Nowhere are snowdrops prettier than on the banks of Mulgrave Old Castle, Sandsend. And on early spring walks in the Forge Valley, or through the woods at Sinnington – another Tabular Hills highlight – popular flowers like wood anemone, wood sorrel, violet and primrose, as well as shyer species like early purple orchid, brush the boots at almost every step.

Local colour

9

The National Park

Since becoming a national park in 1952, the Moors have been in the guardianship of the North York Moors national park authority, composed of local people and others with special expertise. Its original brief, to protect and enhance the landscape and promote appropriate enjoyment of it, has been broadened by a commitment to social vitality.

Supporting these aims is a scheme that pays farmers to restore or maintain traditional features like hedges and stone walls, install stiles, and retain old meadowland. More ambitiously, a 'Moorland Partnership', an alliance of estates and farmers, has attracted EU funds to support sheep farming and grouse shooting. The cash is helping to control bracken, which harbours a tick harmful to grouse and sheep, extend heather-management and subsidise sheep-tick treatment. The rewards will be an improved sheep stock and more shooting days – a double boost for the moorland economy. Visitors, too, will benefit because some 1,500 acres (600 hectares) of heather will be restored and 23,000 acres (9,000 hectares) improved. That spellbinding panorama will be wider and more glorious yet.

Historical Highlights

185–145 million years ago The main rocks of the moors are laid down in Jurassic times when seas invade three times to form a delta. The fossil-rich limestone in the south is created in a shallow coral sea, while the more turbid marine conditions produce widespread sandstones. Deposited in the delta are silts and shales on which roaming dinosaurs leave their footprints, including eight prints that survive in Scalby Bay, near Scarborough. Unearthed from the cliffs, the fossils of several large marine reptiles are now displayed in Whitby Museum.

58–26 million years ago Buckled by the same earth movements that threw up the Alps, the moorland rocks rise slowly from the sea to form a gentle dome.

90,000–10,000BC In the Ice Age, glaciers from Scotland and the Lake District clamp themselves against the Cleveland Hills and Hambleton Hills, with a third, from the North Sea, penetrating Eskdale. As the ice melts c.20,000BC, water overflowing from lakes trapped in Eskdale scours out the gorge of Newton Dale, later adopted by the Whitby–Pickering Railway. The 'Hambleton' ice dams a lake in the Vale of Pickering larger than today's Windermere.

10,000–4000BC The post-glacial moors are invaded by scrub, including heather, followed by a dense hardwood forest. On forays to the moors from settlements by Lake Pickering, the region's first humans, hunters of the Middle Stone Age, begin the destruction of the forest by burning clearings to gain sight of their prey.

3000–1700BC Pastoral nomads of the New Stone Age thinly settle along the southern and western limestone fringe of the Moors. A rare example of their long burial mounds is by the Drove Road above Kepwick.

1700–600BC A population explosion in the Bronze Age has the moor tops, more hospitable than the marshy valleys, almost swarming with people. Practising nomadic cultivation they clear vast tracts of the forest. Their legacy of earthworks, chiefly their hill-top burial mounds and early field systems, is now woven into the fabric of the Moors.

600BC–70AD The iron plough and the 'discovery' of manure lead to a more settled way of life. Traces of Iron Age farmsteads exist on Levisham Moor, near Pickering, where one of Britain's earliest bloomeries, a primitive furnace, has also been found.

70–410AD The Romans establish coastal forts at Saltburn, Goldsborough, near Whitby, Ravenscar, and Scarborough. Preserved at Wheeldale, near Goathland, is a stretch of their road that crossed the Moors from the Roman town of Malton. It probably also served a training camp unique in Britain and rare throughout the Roman Empire – at Cropton, near Pickering, where there is now a waymarked trail.

410–600 The Anglo-Saxons move in. Place names ending in *ing* ('wet land'), *ham* (village), *ton* (township), and *ley* (from 'leah', a clearing), generally indicate their settlements.

626 Lilla Cross is erected on Fylingdales Moor.

867 Vikings sack the abbeys and begin widespread colonisation of the moors. Places whose names end in *by*, Old Norse for 'village', were either founded or taken over by Vikings.

1074 Whitby Abbey is refounded.

1086 Domesday Book records 69 places in the moors, but most of the region has been laid waste by William the Conqueror during his Harrying of the North in 1069.

1132 Rievaulx Abbey is founded directly from France. Twenty-five religious houses are eventually established in or near the Moors. The monks drain and cultivate the valleys but their sheep runs finish off the forest.

1322 Edward II escapes after being routed by the Scots at the Battle of Byland. The following year he returns on a hunting trip, staying at the castles of Pickering, Danby and Whorlton – and in the Merchants' quarters of Rievaulx Abbey's woolhouse, Laskill Farm, Bilsdale.

1538 Rievaulx Abbey is suppressed, followed in 1539 by Byland, Mount Grace, and Whitby.

1577 The first blast furnace in the North of England is erected near Rievaulx. Production ceases in 1647 when the use of wood as fuel is banned.

c1595 Alum working begins at Guisborough. Alum continues to be processed until the last works, at Sandsend, close in 1867.

1619 Beggar's Bridge, Glaisdale, focus of the moors' most romantic legend, is built.

1747 Captain Cook is apprenticed as a seaman at Whitby, on whose colliers he serves for eight years before joining the Royal Navy.

1759 The first turnpike road, linking Whitby with Pickering, opens.

1800 Whitby's first jet workshop opens.

1821 Kirkdale Cave, containing the remains of pre-glacial moorland animals, is discovered near Kirkbymoorside.

1836 Whitby–Pickering railway opens.

1861 Rosedale Ironstone Railway is built. Thirteen Whitby lifeboatmen die on their seventh rescue in one day.

1871 Monkshaven, Whitby's last sailing ship, is launched.

1914 On 16 December, the bombardment of Whitby, Scarborough, and Hartlepool by German battleships gives Britain its first taste of world war. Whitby Abbey is damaged.

1921 The first Forestry Commission trees in the moors are planted at Dalby, near Pickering.

1940 On 3 February, a Heinkel bomber, the first enemy plane shot down on English soil in World War II, crashes at Sleights, near Whitby.

1952 The North York Moors national park is established.

1953 2,000 acres (5,000 hectares) of Farndale is designated a Nature Reserve to prevent visitors uprooting its famous wild daffodils.

1955 The Lyke Wake Walk is devised.

1964 The closure of Skelton Ironstone Mine, just outside the national park, marks the end of an iron industry spanning 2,500 years.

1964–92 Eerily matching the character and spirit of the moors, the three 'golf ball' domes of the Fylingdales Early Warning Station become a popular landmark. Following the commissioning of their 'Pyramid' successor in 1992, the last dome was demolished on 16 June 1994.

1967 Bilsdale TV mast is erected. The dale's vicar observes that 'such monstrosities come to rest in the place of least resistance.'

1969 The Cleveland Way is opened – a 108-mile (174-km) national long-distance trail around the precipitous rim of the national park from Helmsley to Filey. A 48-mile unofficial 'missing link', from Scarborough to Helmsley, now enables the walk to be tackled as a circular route.

1972 Parliament rejects a long-standing scheme to flood Upper Farndale with a reservoir. Rosedale chimney is demolished. Wainwright's Coast to Coast Walk links the North York Moors with the Dales and the Lake District in a 192-mile (309-km) trek from St Bees to Robin Hood's Bay.

1973 Closed in 1965, the Whitby-Pickering Railway is reopened. Approved in 1969, Boulby potash mine begins production.

1974 Most of the 36-mile (58-km) coastline from Saltburn to Scarborough, including 28 miles (45km) within the national park, is designated a Heritage Coast.

1976 Moorland fires destroy 8sq miles (12.8sq km) of heather moor, 4 percent of the total, mainly at the head of Glaisdale and Rosedale. Innovative measures to restore the heather are achieving promising results.

1990 In the area blighted by the Farndale reservoir, the national park introduces payments to farmers for repairing stone walls and buildings and maintaining rights of way and old meadows. The scheme now covers several dales.

1995 Major European Union grants underpin The Moorland Partnership to regenerate the heather moor and sustain the economy.

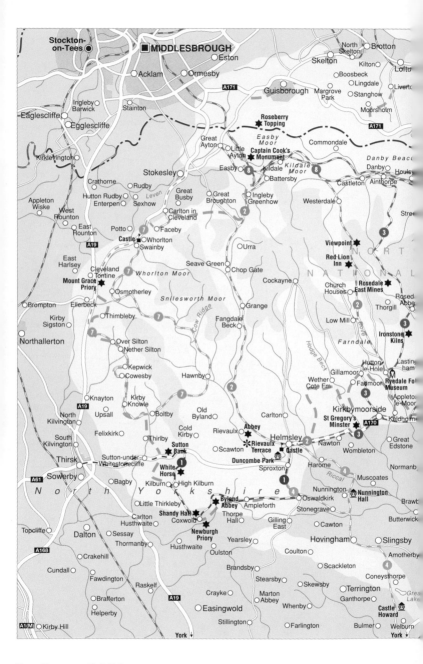

Preceding pages: Hob Hole

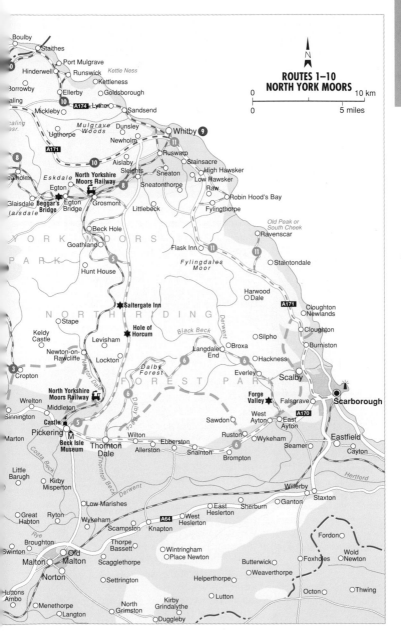

ROUTES 1–10
NORTH YORK MOORS

0 — 10 km

0 — 5 miles

15

Thirsk church details

Route 1

Thirsk – Sutton Bank – Kilburn – Coxwold – Ample-forth – Helmsley (19 miles/30km) *See map, pages 14–15*

From the national park's western gateway this route climbs spectacular Sutton Bank and visits a celebrated country workshop, a literary shrine and two abbeys before reaching the charming market town of Helmsley, headquarters of the national park.

William Wordsworth and his sister Dorothy are among the many travellers who have entered the moors via **Thirsk**. In July 1802 they stayed in the town while journeying to visit William's future wife, Mary Hutchinson, at Brompton, near Scarborough (*see page 36*). In her journal Dorothy notes that when they announced their intention to walk over Sutton Bank, their landlady 'threw out some saucy words in our hearing'.

Herriot's former surgery

The view from Sutton Bank

Off the busy cobbled square, the 15th-century parish church is where vet Alf Wight (1916–95), better known as James Herriot, author of *All Creatures Great and Small*, and his wife were married. With its unusual lacework stone parapet, the church is a good example of the perpendicular style, relatively rare in North Yorkshire. Almost in its shadow is **Herriot's former surgery**, vacated in 1996 when the practice, in which Wight's son Jim is a partner, moved elsewhere. The building is to become a visitor centre devoted largely to the author. Facing it is the **Information Centre**, birthplace of Thomas Lord, who founded Lord's cricket ground in 1787.

Leave Thirsk on the A170 Scarborough road, which soon spirals up ★ **Sutton Bank**. Herriot considered the view from the top, across the Vale of York to the distant Dales, the finest in England. Directly below lies Lake Gormire – 'the wild and (as some people say) bottomless tarn,' as Dorothy Wordsworth described it. The national park information centre on the bank top has leaflets outlining a nature trail down to this glacial lake, and an escarpment walk to the nearby White Horse (*see below*) that passes the **Yorkshire Gliding Club** (*see page 71*).

Take a minor road on the right, descending to the pretty village of **Kilburn**. Oak planks weathering in the open air signal the workshop founded by Robert Thompson (1876–1955), whose successors still produce the much-prized church and domestic oak furniture, signed with Thompson's trademark of a mouse.

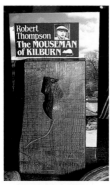

Fondly nicknamed 'Mousey', the founder is said to have carved his first mouse on a church beam when one of his workmen commented that they were as poor as church mice. The trademark is now often said to symbolise 'industry in quiet places'. The firm is still owned by Thompson's family, and his former half-timbered home is part of the **★★ Mouseman Showroom** (open all year except the Christmas holiday, Monday to Thursday 8am–5pm, Friday 8am–3.45pm, Saturday 10am–noon), where furniture is displayed. In his original workshop, now the **★ Mouseman Visitor Centre** (10am–5pm daily, Easter to October; closed Mondays in April, May and October), craftsmen are at work and the story is told of the mouse, found in York Minster and countless other distinguished places.

Making mice in Kilburn

In **Kilburn parish church** a chancel chair is the work of Thompson himself, and a side chapel is furnished by his workshop in his honour.

Proudly overlooking Kilburn is a somewhat larger creature than Thompson's mouse – the hillside **★ White Horse**. Proposed c1800 by villager Thomas Taylor, the giant figure, 312ft (95m) long by 228ft (69m) high, was created in 1857 by volunteers led by schoolmaster John Hodgson. Cut not into chalk but a clay hillside, the horse needs endless grooming to retain his shape and colour – a task undertaken by the local White Horse Association. A byroad leads to a car park from which steps go up to the horse, though he looks far better from a distance.

The White Horse of Kilburn

From Kilburn continue to **Coxwold**. At the entrance to the village is **★ Shandy Hall** (June to September, Wednesday 2–4.30pm and Sunday 2.30–4.30pm, garden daily except Saturday). Shandy is said to be an old Yorkshire term for 'odd'. This is appropriate for what is essentially a 15th-century timber-framed open hall, with bent and massive chimney, that was divided into rooms and encased in brick in the 17th century. The hall was so-named by the clergyman author Laurence Sterne (1713–68) who lived there

Shandy Hall

Cotswold parish church

The Fauconberg motto

Newburgh Priory

while writing most of his comic and sometimes bawdy novel *Tristram Shandy*, followed by *A Sentimental Journey*. A sensation in their day, these books virtually founded the modern novel. The house was restored in the 1960s to become what is regarded as the most unspoiled home of any great English writer. As well as Sterne's study, it contains what he called 'a sweet sitting room' and a wine cellar. Unhappily married, Sterne provided these in the hope that a woman whom he called his 'wife elect' would one day join him at the hall – but she never did.

In 1968, Sterne's bones were brought from a London churchyard and reburied by the door of ★ **Coxwold parish church**. With its striking octagonal tower, this church crowns Coxwold's wide, sloping High Street, where well-kept cottages face neat grass verges. Built c1420, the church still has its original oak ceiling, whose roof bosses include a man sticking out his tongue – a very Shandean image. Sterne himself installed the box pews, though not the unique horseshoe-shaped altar rail. This was designed to leave room for the huge tombs of the Earls of Fauconberg, whose motto, based on the family name Belayse, is worth noting: *Bonne et Belle Assez* – 'To be good and beautiful is enough'. A monument to one of the family shows him in a Roman toga but wearing the curled periwig of his own 17th century – another unwitting 'Shandeism'. The lectern is the work of Austrian sculptor Josef Heu, who found refuge in Coxwold after fleeing the Nazis in 1941. It rests on a stand by Mousey Thompson.

In the 16th century, the Bellayses converted a former Augustinian Priory outside Coxwold into their home. Still lived in by their descendants, ★ **Newburgh Priory** (April to June, Wednesday and Sunday, also Easter and August Bank Holiday Mondays, 2.30–4.45pm), has a tomb that reputedly contains the remains of Oliver Cromwell, one of whose daughters married into the family. A room rav-

aged by a fire in which a maid died remains unrestored because two previous attempts presaged deaths in the family. The Priory has a small but attractive water garden.

In the next village, Wass, the broken wheel window of the west end of ★ **Byland Abbey** (English Heritage, April to September daily 10am–6pm, October daily 10am–4pm) forms a stark and melancholy landmark. Not only was the abbey church, built 1177–97, the largest completed by the English Cistercians in a single task, but the full abbey was the third in this district by the same community. Founded at Byland in 1143, the first was abandoned five years later because nearby Rievaulx Abbey complained of the clash of bells. The 'Byland' monks spent 30 years at Oldstead before moving to the larger site at Wass, though keeping the name Byland, which is 5 miles (8km) away.

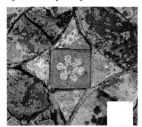

Byland abbey and floor tiles

19

The great west window is believed to have been the model for the Rose Window in York Minster. Scratched as a guide by the mason, the pattern of its centrepiece is still faintly discernible on the inside of the west wall. The abbey has a wealth of glazed floor tiles, and in the so-called Lay Brother's Lane, a passage to the church, survive 35 niche seats occupied by the abbey's lay brothers while waiting to attend service.

Close neighbour to Byland is **Ampleforth Abbey**. Founded in 1802, this is the spiritual heir to Westminster Abbey. For following the suppression of Westminster in 1560, three monks formed a symbolic 'Westminster' community. When one of the three entered a French monastery, this formally took on Westminster's mantle. And the honour was transferred to Ampleforth when a group of monks from the French monastery settled there, in the home of local priest Father Anselm Bolton.

Built between 1924 and 1961 the present ★ **abbey church** (open daily) was designed by Sir Giles Gilbert Scott. Its Gothic appearance conceals a Romanesque interior, where the link with Westminster is marked by a glazed tile from the parent abbey, with a quotation from Isaiah: *Look to the rock from which you were hewn*. The pews were the first major commission of 'Mousey' Thompson, whose later library at the abbey's associated public school is regarded as his masterpiece.

Aspects of Ampleforth

About 30 of the abbey's Benedictine monks teach at the 550-pupil school. Others are engaged in studies or pastoral care, and some run the abbey's 1,000-acre (405-hectare) estate, which includes a dairy herd and Britain's last monastic apple orchard (*see page 67*).

Visitors are welcome in the extensive grounds and the concourse of the modern (1988) Central Building. Linking the abbey and school this includes a tablet marking the site of Father Bolton's house, the cradle of the abbey.

Route 2

Helmsley – Rievaulx Abbey – Bilsdale – Blakey Ridge – Hutton-le-Hole (49 miles/79km) *See map, pages 14–15*

A microcosm of the moors, this route starts at the region's tourist capital, visits the sublime ruin of Rievaulx Abbey, and then links a principal moorland valley with a lofty ridge before calling at a perfect moorland village.

Set at the foot of gentle hills, amid largely pastoral farmland mixed with small woods, ★★ **Helmsley** exudes more the comfortable air of the Cotswolds than the perhaps expected sternness of the North York Moors. A crystal beck hurrying from the hills borders the gardens of creamy limestone cottages, overlooked by the pinnacled tower of the parish church and the shattered keep of the 12th-century castle. Plentifully supplied with good shops and galleries, not to mention a working smithy specialising in ornamental ironwork, the town hinges on its wide Market Place, dominated by a canopied Victorian statue of the second Earl of Feversham. Incorporated in **The Black Swan**, a premier hostelry of the moors, is a fine 15th-century timbered house that was once occupied by the agent of the Duke of Rutland. In July 1802, William Wordsworth and his sister Dorothy stayed at Helmsley on their way to see William's future wife, Mary Hutchinson, at Brompton, near Scarborough. 'We slept at a very nice inn and were well treated,' Dorothy notes in her journal. The inn was most probably the former Golden Lion, now a butcher's shop on the corner of the Market Place.

Feversham dominates the square

Helmsley Castle

Trade generated by Rievaulx Abbey (*see page 22*) is probably what brought Helmsley into being. It grew up with the shelter of its **castle** (English Heritage, April to

September daily 10am–6pm, for winter times tel: 01439 770442). Begun about 1186 by Robert de Roos, whose descendants now live at Belvoir Castle, Derbyshire, it marks a transition from the early concept of a castle as a series of defences to a fortress of all round strength. The keep, slighted after a siege of 1644, is not in the castle's centre but its outer wall. Ultimately, as in castles like Conway, there would be no keep at all. Helmsley's castle is also notable for its interlocking earthworks and a well-preserved Tudor range, home of the Helmsley squires until replaced by Duncombe Park. In late spring the castle walls arc adorned with the starlike pink flowers of fairy foxglove, a rare alpine plant. Its seeds were sown here by botanist Sir Walter Acheson in the 1930s.

The keep

Alexander Pope (1688–1744) was scornful of the sale that led to the building of ★★ **Duncombe Park** (June to September daily; April, May and October Saturday to Wednesday; 11am–4.30pm). 'Helmsley, once proud Buckingham's delight, slides to a scrivener or a city knight,' he scoffed. The knight was Sir Charles Duncombe, a London banker, who bought the estate on the death of the rakish second Duke of Buckingham in 1689. Sir Charles lived in Helmsley Castle, but his nephew-heir Thomas Browne, who took the name Duncombe, commissioned the baroque-style Duncombe Park in 1713. Its amateur architect, William Wakefield, squire of Huby, near York, may have been helped by Sir John Vanbrugh, at that time working on Castle Howard (*see page 30*). In 1845, wings designed by Sir Charles Barry, architect of the Houses of Parliament, were added. Though these survive, the main house is a Victorian rebuild following two fires. The original design was faithfully copied – with the addition of two fire escapes disguised as towers. The hall's 5½-acre (2.5-hectare) Victorian **walled garden** (daily 11am–5pm) is currently being restored.

Duncombe Park inside and out

For 60 years the hall was leased as a girls' school. However, in 1985 the present Earl Feversham, a descendant of Thomas Browne, moved back. The house is now a showcase both for many original Duncombe treasures and contemporary local craftsmanship, like the superb dining table made by Eric Gott, of Pickering. The grounds offer extensive walks, by the Rye and in woodland which, designated a National Nature Reserve in 1994, contains Britain's tallest lime tree (148ft/48m). A yew tunnel delights children, and there is a pioneering (c.1718) example of a ha-ha, a landscape device to provide a stockproof boundary that doesn't disrupt the view.

Garden statuary

High above a bend of the Rye, a wide grass terrace with temples was originally linked by a carriage drive to a similar terrace above Rievaulx Abbey – an outstanding piece of romantic landscape architecture.

Rievaulx Abbey

Bilsdale from Newgate Bank

Leaving Helmsley on the B1257 Stokesley road, the route takes the first sideroad. Signposted Scawton, it leads to ★★★ **Rievaulx Abbey** (English Heritage, April to September daily 10am–6pm, October to March 10am–4pm). The now supremely beautiful setting was viewed as 'a place of horror and waste solitude' by the abbey's 12 founder monks, who arrived direct from France in 1132. Larger than Fountains Abbey, Rievaulx was both the first and biggest Cistercian abbey in the North of England. At its 13th-century peak it housed 150 monks and 500 lay brothers, 'so that the church swarmed with them like a hive with bees'. At the 1538 Dissolution only 22 monks remained, and the huge dormitory was a grain store. Because of the abbey's narrow site, between steep banks of the Rye, the church was aligned north-south. Its greatest glory is its chancel, c1230. Standing to its full height, with two tiers of lancet windows above cluster-column arches, it is a majestic example of the Early English style.

Building stone was ferried along a canal linked to the river Rye. A short footpath to Bow Bridge, north of the abbey, runs by the shallow bed of the canal, one of Britain's earliest industrial waterways. In 1577, the first blast furnace in the North of England sprang up here, though its exact site hasn't been located.

Passing two thatched cottages, the road climbs to rejoin the B1257. Here is access to the ★★ **Rievaulx Terrace and Temples** (National Trust, late March to October daily 10.30am–6pm or dusk). The climax of that carriage ride from Duncombe Park, the half-mile terrace was created in 1758 by Thomas Browne to obtain exquisite views of the ruined abbey. Furnished as a banqueting house, one of its two temples is open to the public.

A short way along the B1257, ★★ **Newgate Bank** commands a superb view up the 12-mile (19-km) length of Bilsdale, and across to the more richly-wooded upper Ryedale. Not even the Bilsdale 1,022-ft (340-m) TV mast can spoil this classic picture of rural England. **Laskill Farm**, at the foot of the hill, was the wool house of Rievaulx Abbey. In 1323 Edward II slept in its merchants' quarters during a hunting trip.

Steeped in tradition midway along Bilsdale is the thatched ★ **Spout House** (Easter to October daily except Thursday 10am–4pm). Built in the 16th century, this is believed to be the oldest cottage in the Moors on its original site. For long doubling as the Sun Inn (but still known as 't'Spout'), it was occupied until 1914, when it was replaced by the present inn alongside. A visit reveals its 'cruck' construction, a timber-frame method practised from Saxon times to the 18th century. There is also much history relating to the Bilsdale Hunt, founded in the 17th

Spout House

century and strongly associated with Spout House. A huntsman's grave by the door of the present inn was erected there after the vicar objected to its hunting motifs. Owned and run by the Ainsley family since 1823, the inn is the least-changed traditional pub in the moors. Completely isolated, it even fields its own cricket team, once the subject of a BBC documentary, *Cricket at the Spout*.

Just off the main road at nearby Fangdale Beck, a **telephone box** has been painted green ever since Lord Feversham insisted on that harmonious colour as a condition of the box being installed in the 1930s. In 1992 British Telecom caused outrage by replacing the listed green box with a modern type. The company was fined £3,000 and ordered to reinstate a traditional box – in green.

Ever green

The curious name of the next village, **Chop Gate**, means 'pedlars' way', 'chop' being derived from the Old Norse word for pedlar, *ceap*. From the village the road climbs Clay Bank to **another fine view**, across the Vale of Cleveland, with the peak of Roseberry Topping prominent. The Cleveland Way, Coast to Coast Walk and Lyke Wake Walk (*see page 40*) all cross here.

23

Leave the B1257 for **Ingleby Greenhow**. Soon visible on the hillside is the 1-in-3 Ingleby Incline, the bold lift-off from the Cleveland Plain of the Rosedale Ironstone Railway (*see page 26*). In Ingleby Greenhow's mainly **Georgian church**, the quaint carvings of animals and birds on top of Norman pillars might be the work of a 19th-century vicar who was fond of carving stones.

Captured in stone

Hob Hole

After driving through the villages of Battersby, with its fine Tudor Old Hall, and Kildale, turn right for Westerdale. On reaching the moor top, this road brings a ★★★ **matchless panorama** of moor-and-dale. Against a dipping foreground of heather, the entire horizon is filled with interlocking ridges and dales, over which trail the characteristic little moorland roads. The road drops to the green hollow of Hob Hole, a picnic place whose ford often features in pictures of the Milk Race and vintage car rallies.

At the crossroads in Westerdale go straight on, turning right when joining the Castleton–Hutton-le-Hole road. Here stands the cross ★ **Young Ralph**, the national park's emblem (*see page 63*). His stockier neighbour Old Ralph is just beyond the slight hump of heather to the west. Erected in the late 18th century, Young Ralph perhaps indicated a new line in the moorland trackways.

Refreshment at the Lion Inn

Heading for Hutton-le-Hole, with Rosedale opening out on the left, the route passes the lonely ★ **Lion Inn** (*see page 68*). With its massively-beamed interior, this perhaps originated as a wayside alehouse to earn money for an order of Friars that in 1348 had a chapel near this unlikely spot. In the 18th and early 19th centuries it was sustained by traffic in lime and coal. Cockpit Howe, a hollowed-out burial mound by the pub, is so named because cockfights were staged there.

Past the Lion, turn right and descend to **Farndale**. At Church House, the Feversham Arms is a good walkers' pub, with flagstone floor and old range. The lane alongside is the start, or finish, of the famous 1½-mile (2.5-km) ★★ **daffodil walk**. Wild daffodils bloom throughout the 7-mile (11-km) valley. Though some say they were planted by Rievaulx monks, and others claim the seed was sown by an itinerant 17th-century Roman Catholic monk named Nicholas Postgate, their origin is a mystery.

Hutton-le-Hole

If the plan to flood Upper Farndale with a reservoir hadn't been thrown out by Parliament in 1972, the next part of the route, across the river Dove and up steep Monket Bank, would have been obliterated by the dam. At the bank top, turn left and drive to Low Mill, the other end of the daffodil walk, and thence to ★★★ **Hutton-le-Hole**. With its limestone cottages scattered around hummocky sheep-cropped greens, and a beck spanned by white-painted footbridges, Hutton is the most 'picture-postcard' village of the moors. Its present appearance derives from the 17th and 18th centuries, when most of its cottages were built by Quaker weavers. The best known Quaker-weaver, John Richardson, lived at what is now Quaker Cottage. Becoming a missionary, he won fame in America by travelling 4,000 miles on a white horse.

Ryedale folk exhibits

In the 19th century, Hutton had a more rumbustious period as a lodging centre for Rosedale miners. Their entertainment included frequent bare knuckle fights. Today's top attraction is the ★★ **Ryedale Folk Museum** (Easter to October 10am–5.30pm, February and November for booked parties), the premier museum of moorland life. Reconstructed in its 2½-acre (1-hectare) grounds are several vernacular buildings, including a cruck cottage and an Elizabethan manor house. The cottage has its 'witch post', a pillar of rowan standing between door and hearth to ward off evil spirits. Transferred from Rosedale is Britain's best preserved medieval glass furnace, monument to a brief 16th-century period when Huguenot glassmakers settled in the area. The museum hosts craft demonstrations and each September stages the 'World Championship' of Merrills, an ancient peg-board game once popular in the moors.

John Bunting's mechanic

From Hutton, the Kirkbymoorside road leads to the A170 for the return to Helmsley. Built into the garage at **Nawton**, the **sculpted figure** of a car mechanic clutching his spanner is by John Bunting, a distinguished contemporary sculptor who lives locally (*see page 30*). Beneath the fenced-off portion of a field opposite Pockley, a Roman villa, uncovered in 1966, awaits excavation.

Helmsley – Kirkbymoorside – Rosedale – mid-Eskdale – Lastingham (54 miles/87km) *See map, pages 14–15*

In highly-scenic settings, ancient churches and ironstone feature prominently in this route, which also introduces beautiful Eskdale.

Leave by the A170 Scarborough road, and after passing through Nawton take a minor road straight ahead where the main road bears right. Off this lane, in the sheltered gorge of Kirkdale, is ★★ **St Gregory's Minister**, an isolated Saxon church. A Minster is a 'mission house', and one existed here long before the present church was built in 1055. The crude inscription on a 7-ft (2-m) Saxon sundial, the most complete of its kind in the world, tells how, when the church was 'all tobrocan and to falan,' it was 'bohte' by an earl named Orm, who had it 'made anew from grund'. The inscription even identifies the mason and priest at the time – Haward and Brand – making them the earliest craftsman and parish priest known by name in Yorkshire. Though largely rebuilt in the 19th century, the church also retains its original wall benches, origin of the phrase 'the weakest go to the wall'. John Betjeman read poems from the pulpit in 1970.

St Gregory portraits

In 1821, quarrymen blasting the roadside cliff near the church opened up a window on the past. The Kirkdale Cave contained the bones and teeth of animals such as hippopotamus, rhinoceros, brown bear, bison, lion, and straight-tusked elephant. Residents of what was to be the moors after the Ice Age, they had been dragged there by hyenas. The cave was destroyed, but its relics are in the Yorkshire Museum at York.

Continue on the minor road to rejoin the A170, then leave this road to enter ★**Kirkbymoorside**. Its unspoilt little centre contrasts pleasantly with the clutter of garages and factories by the main road. **Buckingham House**, near the top of the main street, is reputedly where Helmsley's rollicking Duke of Buckingham died after catching pneumonia while hunting in 1687 with the Bilsdale Hounds, the pack he founded as perhaps the earliest hunt in England. In the nearby **High Hall**, treasures of Tutankhamen's tomb were catalogued in the 1920s, when the hall was owned by the brother of Egyptologist Howard Carter.

Drive to Gillamoor, turning right at the Royal Oak. Sundial addicts will stop at Dial House, in front of which is possibly England's **most complex sundial**. It bears out Hilaire Belloc's couplet:

England's most complex sundial

I am a sundial and I make a botch
Of what's done far better by a watch

Ironstone kilns in Rosedale

The remains of Rosedale Abbey

Lealholm: Sir Francis' insignia

By the church, a plaque in the wall praises the sudden **surprise view of Farndale**.

At the foot of the bank keep right and continue to Hutton-le-Hole (*see page 24*). Take the Lastingham road but fork left to Rosedale Abbey. The road descends to the village via the 1-in-3 Chimney Bank, so called because an ironstone-mine chimney, a popular landmark, stood here from 1861 to 1972. Still there, left of bank top, is a row of ★★ **ironstone kilns**. Their purpose was to roast, or calcine, the ore, reducing its moisture content and thus the royalties payable to the landowner.

Transforming Rosedale into the Klondyke of the moors, the valley's ironstone boom began in 1856 when the first of four mines opened. Rows of cottages sprang up to house the increasing numbers of miners. The cottages at bank top were occupied by employees of the railway, which terminated here. Opened in 1861 to transport the ore to blast furnaces in the North East, the railway ran for 11 miles on the roof of the moors. Crossing gills and valley heads on huge embankments of clinker, it plunged to the Cleveland Plain via the mile-long (1.5-km) rope-worked Ingleby Incline. Probably no other standard gauge railway in Britain operated over such a distance in such hostile terrain. Special snowploughs built for the line incorporated a stove and bunk beds. The end came in 1929, three years after the closure of Rosedale's East Mines, the last in production (*see page 28*).

To build schools and chapels the miners plundered the ruins of **Rosedale Abbey** – a small nunnery. Today's only standing fragment, a truncated tower, is obscurely located down a footpath from the church, over whose north door an inscribed stone from the abbey bears the apt legend: 'Omnia Vanitas' – All Is Vanity.

From Rosedale Abbey take the Egton Bridge road. This soon becomes a fine drive over open moor. Near where the road crosses Bluewath Beck is one of the few **peat diggings** in the moors. Some householders in Glaisdale still exercise their common right to cut the peat for fuel.

Beyond the beck, fork left to ★ **Lealholm**. A good place to stop, this Esk Valley village has a riverside green, pub by an anglers' pool, shop, tearoom, and popular plant nursery. A set of stepping stones is the key to a 10-minute circuit of the village. Lealholm's character owes a lot to Sir Francis Ley, a Nottingham lace maker, and his wife Alyson, who were Lords of the Manor early this century. Lady Ley planted the numerous specimen trees, and her husband built model cottages. Together with the elegant stone alcoves of former public taps – the village's first piped water – these bear Sir Francis's insignia. The Leys laid out Crunkley Gill, a glacial gorge, with public paths

nd scats, but a 1930 flood destroyed their handiwork. The
heights of that flood and others are engraved on the wall
of the Methodist Chapel, by the stepping stones.

Now take the Danby road. Beyond the hamlet of Houl-
syke, the nearly-blank north wall of Danby Castle (*see be-
ow*) draws the eye on the south hillside. Turning a corner
by the medieval **Duck Bridge**, named after the mason who
restored it in the 18th century, the road reaches Danby
Lodge, a former shooting lodge that is now the **Moors
Centre** (April to November daily 10am–5pm, November to March weekends 11am–4pm). The main showcase
for the national park, this is also the starting point for a variety of waymarked walks. Nearby **Danby village** has a
★ **working water mill** (Easter to October Wednesday to
Sunday 10.30am–5.30pm).

If the mill is visited, continue past the adjacent railway station, forking left at the **Fox and Hounds** in
Ainthorpe (*see page 68*). Otherwise, from the Moors Centre, return to Duck Bridge, cross the concrete causeway
alongside, and turn left up a narrow lane.

Both routes lead to ★ **Danby Castle** (closed to the public, but a leaflet is available at the Moors Centre). Built
in the 14th century, the castle was home to Catherine Parr,
sixth and last wife of Henry VIII. She lived there with
William Latimer, who died the year before she became
queen in 1543. The castle has peculiarly-angled corner
towers. One of these is now the living room, with bed-
rooms above, of Danby Castle Farm, which long ago
adopted the ruin. The original parlour, with fine oak pan-
elling, is behind the upper storey of the range facing the
road. Each October it is the setting of Danby Court Leet
(*see page 65*), a manorial court administering common
rights on the 14,000-acre (5,700-hectare) Danby Estate,
owned by Lord Downe, of Wykeham near Scarborough.

Duck Bridge near Danby

Danby's water mill

Danby Castle

The castle guards the entrance to Little Fryup Dale, whose name is probably derived from the Old English word *hop*, meaning a remote enclosed place. At its head, which certainly is remote and enclosed, take a road that goes straight up the moor. At a T junction turn left, for Rosedale Abbey. On the descent, opportunity can be taken to visit the ★★ **Rosedale East Mines**. More spectacular than those at Bank Top, they are reached from a side road signposted Dale Head. The half-mile (0.8-km) path to them, mainly on the old railway, starts opposite a row of cottages near a converted chapel.

From Rosedale Abbey head for Cropton (*see page 67*), but at the foot of its bank take the road to ★★ **Lastingham**. Embosomed in trees, the lovely village is a far cry from the wilderness that greeted St Cedd, a missionary from Lindisfarne, when he arrived here in AD655. His abbey was founded among what Bede called 'high and remote hills, which seemed more suitable for the dens of robbers and haunts of wild beasts than for human habitation'. Though Cedd's abbey vanished from history two centuries later, when it was probably sacked by Danes, in 1078 a Whitby abbot began building a new monastery at the same site. Viking raiders wrecked his plan, but not before completion of the ★★★ **abbey's crypt**. A church in its own right, with chancel, nave, side aisles, vaulted roof on fat Norman pillars, and altar probably marking the grave of St Cedd, this crypt survives beneath the present church. Pevsner hails it as 'unforgettable...representing the 11th century at the highest level'.

Lastingham church and crypt

A start was also made on the abbey's chancel. Its pillars and semi-circular apse became the nucleus of the present church, built c.1230. The nave of the monastery would have extended beyond the church's west end, whose protruding pillars would have carried the abbey's transept.

The church once had an unusual link with the attractive **Blacksmith's Arms** facing. An 18th-century curate played his fiddle in the pub – after the Sunday service. He replied to the inquiring Archdeacon by pointing out the difficulty of supporting his wife and 13 children on an annual stipend of £20. 'Give me £20 more and I will eschew the alehouse, and my children will bless you,' he wrote. The Archdeacon probed no further.

The Blacksmith's Arms

From Lastingham, return to the A170 for Helmsley via Spaunton and **Appleton-le-Moors**. With its pencil-thin spire, Appleton Church was designed in 1863 by J.L. Pearson, architect of Truro Cathedral. Paid for by the widow of a local shipowner, it was a memorial to her husband who died while riding his horse in the main street. On a cottage at the far end, three weathered faces are said to be the Three Bloodsuckers – doctor, lawyer, parson.

Helmsley – Nunnington – Hovingham – Castle Howard
(22 miles/35km) *See map, pages 14–15*

Forsaking the Moors for the rolling, richly-wooded
Howardian Hills, designated an area of outstanding natural beauty immediately south of the national park, this
route links three country houses, climaxing with the ma-
estic Castle Howard.

From Helmsley take the A170 Scarborough road, but very
soon turn right to Harome, from where Nunnington is signposted along pleasant byways. Built of mellow sandstone
in the early 17th century, and extensively altered just under a century later, ★★ **Nunnington Hall** (National Trust,
June to August daily except Monday 1–5.30pm, other
months April to October daily except Monday and Friday 2–6pm) is a perfect small country manor house. Seen
from the nearby bridge over the river Rye, from where
its Tudor west front, with dormer windows and massive
chimney stacks, stands behind a wide trout pool over-leant
by a weeping willow, Nunnington Hall is an English ex-
ile's dream of home.

Nunnington Hall and coat-of-arms

29

Before the hall was built, one of the squires of Nunnington was Sir Thomas Parr, whose daughter Catherine
was the sixth and last wife of Henry VIII, the only wife
to survive him (*see page 27*). The hall's main builder,
the first Viscount Preston, was secretary to James II (who
ruled 1685–88). For plotting against William of Orange,
who won the throne after James fled, Preston served a spell
in the Tower of London. His epitaph in Nunnington church
states: 'Unsuccessful in Serving an Earthly Prince he ded-
icated the remainder of his days to a pious retirement and
the Service of the King of Heaven'. For a while, the hall
was owned by Preston's sister, Mary. She was so fat that
in her old age she couldn't walk across the room and with
her coffin weighed 80 stone (1,120lb).

The hall's main architectural features are its magnificent oak-panelled hall, wide oak staircase, and flagged
'Stone Hall', the kitchen of Viscount Preston's day. An
added attraction is a fascinating collection of 'miniatures'
– tiny buildings, rooms and craftsmen's workshops, all
perfect at one-eighth scale. The hall's walled garden has
an old orchard and flower-rich meadow with mown paths.
Tea can be taken by the Rye.

From Nunnington drive to Hovingham over Caulkleys
Bank, a good viewpoint for the Vale of Pickering. The
direct way is up the sycamore-lined hill beyond Nunnington Bridge, but a short detour can be made through

The walled garden

Nunnington village. Work on view at **Nunnington Stu-dios** (all year Tuesday to Sunday plus Bank Holidays 11am–5pm) includes sculpture by John Bunting (*see page 24*), a frequent exhibitor at the Royal Academy.

Set around an irregular green, **Hovingham** is a spick and span estate village. The imposing gatehouse of its ★ **hall** (closed except garden occasionally for charity) is right on the street. Horses were a prime consideration when Sir Thomas Worsley built the hall c.1745–55. The cavernous space glimpsed through the gatehouse was a Riding Hall, where horsemanship could be practised or demonstrated before spectators in a viewing gallery. The other central ground-floor rooms were stables, with the living rooms, and even the ballroom above. But the hall wasn't quite as grand as Sir Thomas planned, and its garden front bears his epitaph: 'He built according to his means, not his wishes'. The hall is still occupied by the Worsleys, and it was the home of Katherine Worsley, the present Duchess of Kent, before her marriage in 1961.

30

'Hail Castle Howard!'

Perhaps Sir Thomas aimed to outdo ★★★ **Castle Howard**. Signposted off the Malton road, this palatial house (mid-March to early November, grounds from 10am, house from 11am) inspired John Betjeman to write: 'Hail Castle Howard! Hail Vanbrugh's noble dome, Where Yorkshire in her splendour rivals Rome!' The first sight of the dome, crowning the huge house spread along the crest of hill beyond the great lake, is indeed breathtaking. The more so when it is realised that this was the very first building designed by Sir John Vanbrugh (1644–1726).

Entrusted with the commission by the 3rd Earl of Carlisle through their common membership of London's dilettante Kit Kat Club, how could Vanbrugh, playwright, former soldier and son of a confectioner, be sure that the palace he roughly sketched would stand up?

The practicalities were probably in the sound hands of Nicholas Hawksmoor, a protégé of Sir Christopher Wren, whom Vanbrugh engaged as his 'Clerk of Works'. After Vanbrugh's death in 1726, Hawksmoor alone designed the magnificent **Mausoleum**, one of the many outstanding buildings in the grounds. Members of the Howard family, from which the great house and surrounding hills get their name, are still interred there.

Erected mostly in the years 1730–37, the house was nevertheless unfinished on the 3rd Earl's death in 1738. The west wing, designed by his son-in-law Thomas Robinson, wasn't added until 1750. By that time, the flamboyant baroque style, in which the earliest part of the house was built, had fallen out of favour. Built in the much more restrained Palladian style, Robinson's wing is widely disparaged for spoiling the symmetry of Castle Howard. But

to many visitors the main room of this wing, the **Long Gallery**, is the most appealing in the house.

The centrepiece of the entire house is the marble-floored Hall, rising to the magnificent 70-ft (21-m) dome, across which charge great 'Horses of the Sun'. With vaulted vistas down passageways, and glimpses of staircases, the effect is highly theatrical; and Vanbrugh had designed stage scenery! The principal rooms contain paintings by Gainsborough, Reynolds, Rubens and others, and furniture by Sheraton and Chippendale, while the Pre-Raphaelite chapel has stained glass by Burne-Jones. In the parkland, a lovely walk along a terrace leads to the elegant **Chapel of the Four Winds**, from which a return can be made by the shore of the south lake. A rose garden created in 1974 by the late George Howard in memory of his wife now has more than 300 varieties.

Queen Victoria spent two days at Castle Howard in 1850. She alighted at the estate's own railway station, where the Howards retained the right to stop any train, even an express, until the outbreak of World War II. Such was the power of the mighty Howards, who once even had their own army. But following the death of the 9th Earl of Carlisle in 1911, the estates were divided, with the titled arm of the family receiving a Cumbrian portion based on Naworth Castle, near Carlisle, where the 13th Earl of Carlisle now resides. Castle Howard is presently occupied by the Hon. Simon Howard and his wife Annette.

During the summer months the castle provides a splendid backdrop for concerts held in the grounds, usually but not always classical. Pavarotti is just one of many stars to have performed here.

To return to Helmsley, use the B1257 to its junction with the A170. Facing the junction is Duncombe Park's huge Tuscan-arched Nelson Gate, erected to commemorate Nelson's victory at Trafalgar in 1805.

The Long Gallery

Chapel of the Four Winds

Allegories abound

Steaming up in Grosmont

Route 5

Pickering – Hole of Horcum – Goathland – Grosmont
(21 miles/34km) *See map, pages 14–15*

From the headquarters of the North Yorkshire Moors Railway at Pickering to the line's operational centre and northern terminus at Grosmont, this route explores the countryside around the railway – a major attraction.

Pickering: parish church and wall painting detail

With its two principal streets rising unerringly to the large parish church, which remains aloof from both due to flights of steps and passageways, **Pickering** is a town of strong character. Not a little of this character stems from the railway, whose **station** stands at the bottom of one of those streets – Market Place. A strong feature in its own right, the station brings the Moors Railway steam trains into the heart of the town.

But first the ★ **parish church**. With its 14th-century spire, a landmark across Pickering's eponymous Vale, this contains probably Britain's most extensive set of medieval wall paintings. Dating from the 15th century, they cover both sides of the nave with Biblical scenes and events such as the murder of Thomas a Becket. Carefully restored after being discovered under whitewash in 1851, their purpose was to instruct the faithful at a time when few could read. Tablets in the church commemorate the Pickering surveyors who helped plan the US capital, Washington, DC, and William Marshall (1745–1818), an apostle of organised farming. His Board of Agriculture, set up in 1793, was the forerunner of the modern Ministry.

In his home, Beck Isle, Marshall ran a farmers' school – the first college of agriculture. The charming Gothic-windowed building is now home to the ★★ **Beck Isle**

Museum of Rural Life (late March to October 10am–
pm). Here can be seen the ★★ photographs of Sydney
Smith (1884–1956). Working in the tradition of Whitby's
Frank Sutcliffe (*see page 51*), with whom his career over-
lapped, Smith was a Pickering commercial photographer
who took pictures of local scenes and characters for his
own pleasure. These are now a most beautiful record of
rural England in the first half of the 20th century.

In 1106 Henry I designated the extensive woodland
around Pickering as the 'Honour and Forest of Pickering'
, vast Royal hunting forest. As its capital, ★ Pickering
Castle (English Heritage, April to September daily 10am–
5pm, for winter opening tel: 01751 770442) entertained
virtually every British monarch for the next 300 years.
William the Conqueror probably stayed there, for after lay-
ing waste most of the North in 1069, he kept land at Pickering, where he might well have founded the castle.
Together with much surrounding countryside, this remains
a Crown property, part of the Duchy of Lancaster. The castle's chief features are the c.1220 keep on its large mound
and its unusually well-preserved outer walls, built
1323–26. One of several towers is named after Rosamund
de Clifford. Mother of an illegitimate son to Henry II
(1133–1189), she was poisoned by the King's wife.

Ideally starting at the railway station, the route leaves Pickering by the A169 Whitby road. Open moor is reached
spectacularly at the mile-wide (1.5-km) ★★ Hole of Horcum, by Saltersgate Bank. Amazingly, moorland springs
sculpted this impressive amphitheatre, but in legend it is
either the Devil's Punchbowl or the outcome of a fit of
rage by a local giant, Wade. Angry with his wife one day,
he grabbed a handful of earth and flung it at her. The proof
is not only the Hole but the nearby rounded hill of Blakey
Topping – the thrown earth. Put up in 1975, an engraved
stone at the bank top immortalises a farmer's battle against
what the inscription calls 'planning official intrigue'. A
path into the Hole can be linked with another around its
rim to form an excellent 7-mile (11-km) walk, with a stop
at The Horseshoe, a good pub in Levisham.

In the ★ Saltersgate Inn, at the foot of the bank, still
burns a fire that reputedly hasn't gone out for two centuries. Legend has it that in 1796 a band of smugglers mur-
dered a Customs' officer, burying his body beneath the
hearth. To make sure this would never be disturbed, they
invented a yarn in which local people, tormented by the
Devil, pushed the Devil on to the inn's fire. It must be kept
burning to prevent him escaping to make more mischief.

The inn's real history hardly needs dressing up. Originally a roadside cottage, it became an inn in the 18th century when the Earl of Mulgrave's coachman suggested

Beck Isle Museum: interior

A historic view of the castle

33

Hole of Horcum

The new-look Fylingdales

Visitors and church in Goathland

Roman Road sign

stabling horses there to speed the Earl's frequent journey between Whitby and Pickering. Through its remote location the inn became a clearing house for smuggled goods, chiefly brandy and silk but also salt, which had passed this way since monastic times – hence the name.

Brutally dominating the way ahead is the so-called 'pyramid' of the **Fylingdales Early Warning Station**, which replaced the famous trio of 'golf balls' in 1992. A bit like huge archery targets, the roundels on its three faces consist of thousands of tiny radar antennae. They scan for missiles, satellites and other objects.

At Ellerbeck Bridge, where the main road dips to a stream, a short track on the left leads to ★ **Fen Bog**. The remnants of a post-glacial swamp, this is a popular place to photograph trains of the Moors Railway as they enter or leave Newton Dale (*see page 34*). Like the track by the Warning Station, which leads to the ancient **Lilla Cross** (*see page 62*), this is part of the Lyke Wake Walk.

Beyond Ellerbeck, fork left to Goathland. En route, the Moors Railway is encountered again at **Moorgates**, another good viewpoint.

A bracing moorland village, ★ **Goathland** has become highly popular in recent years as the setting of the BBC drama series Heartbeat. Many hope it will one day regain its former relaxed air of a small inland spa – which is virtually what it is. For although Whitby Abbey established a hermitage in what became known as God's Land – hence *Goathland* – there was nothing but a handful of cottages by the church until the railway station opened in 1865. Hotels and large houses then spread quickly along the mile (1.5km) or so of common between the station (at the then-isolated corn mill) and the **church**. This expansion led to the rebuilding of the church in 1895. Containing much fine craftsmanship in stone and wood, including work by 'Mousey' Thompson (*see page 17*), this is a notable building by celebrated York architect Walter Brierley (1852–1926) – the 'Lutyens of the North.' Unearthed during the building of the church, and now in its chancel, is a stone slab incised with crosses. This could be the altar of the original hermitage.

A mile beyond the church, in Wheeldale, is the ★★ **Roman Road** (*see page 10*). Locals call this Wade's Causeway. The ubiquitous giant is said to have built it for his wife, who kept a cow on the moors. Within the village, short paths lead to the waterfalls of Mallyan Spout and Water Ark, the latter in a mini amphitheatre crossed by the Moors Railway. This again features at **Darnholme**, a delightful stepping-stoned hollow. But most exquisite is ★★★ **Beck Hole**, a hamlet with an arc of cottages fronting a little green raised like a dais. Quoits (*see page 65*) is most elightfully played here, inquests afterwards being conducted in the **Birch Hall Inn**, where beer is served through a hatch in a flag-floored bar adorned with quoiting pictures. Don't miss the Victorian oil painting clamped to the pub's outside wall, a gift of its Royal Academician artist Sir Algernon Newton, who lived in the hamlet. Likewise, don't miss the ★ **view** from the hill near the railway bridge.

The Birch Hall Inn

From Goathland take the A169 towards Whitby, but turn off for **Grosmont**. Its priory and ironworks are long gone, but Grosmont now bustles with visitors to the 18-mile (29-km) ★★★ **North Yorkshire Moors Railway**.

Except for an 1830 extension to Middlesbrough of the Stockton and Darlington Railway, which opened in 1825, the Whitby Pickering Railway, completed in 1836, was Yorkshire's first passenger line. Its engineer was the S&DR's George Stephenson – but he didn't distinguish himself here. Stephenson's route not only required a rope-worked incline between Beck Hole and Goathland, it also had such tight curves that when express trains were introduced from London special carriages had to be made. The initial motive power was the horse, pulling coach-like carriages. When steam was introduced in 1846, the locos could work only up to each end of the Beck Hole incline. Carriages and freight wagons were lowered or raised against the counterbalancing weight of trucks loaded with water tanks. Charles Dickens, a passenger in 1844, later wrote of 'that curious railroad by the Whitby moor, so much the more curious in that you were balanced against a counterweight of water, and you did it like Blondin.' A 4-mile (6.5-km) deviation, from Grosmont to Moorgates, eliminated the incline in 1865.

Nostalgia in Grosmont

35

The first three miles of the deviation, including the incline, are now a popular 'Historical Rail Trail' linking Grosmont and Goathland. Ideally varied with a call at Beck Hole, this can be combined with a train ride in the opposite direction, over the prettiest part of the line. At Grosmont visitors to the engine shed can see locomotives undergoing restoration or being prepared for duty and walk through the narrow castellated tunnel used by Stephenson's horse-drawn trains. The line's most dramatic feature is that great gorge of **Newton Dale**. Not penetrated by public roads, and with sheer cliffs up to 400ft (121m) high, this moorland version of the Grand Canyon was scoured by the overflow from glacial lakes in Eskdale.

The line established Whitby as a resort. For when 'Railway King' George Hudson bought it in 1845, he embarked on developing Whitby's West Cliff. Axed by Beeching in 1965, it reopened just eight years later – the fulfilment of a heroic, and initially derided, voluntary effort led by local man Tom Salmon.

Steaming through Newton Dale

Route 6

Pickering – Forge Valley – Dalby Forest (3? miles/56km) *See map, pages 14–15*

A national nature reserve and scenic forest drive are high lights of this route, which also has intriguing literary and aviation interest.

From Pickering (*see page 32*) take the A170 Scarbor ough road. Usually running a little north of this busy artery the national park boundary crosses it to embrace **Thornton-le-Dale**. Though not instantly today appearing to be 'Yorkshire's Prettiest Village', this dubious accolade from 1908 has contributed to Thornton becoming one of the North York Moors busiest honeypots. But it undoubtedly has its charms.

Thornton-le-Dale

36

Its most celebrated feature, by a bend in the stream that ripples attractively through the village, is a thatched **chocolate-box cottage**, a former bailiff's home that often appears on travel posters. The path to it, off the main street, leads to more pretty rose-clad cottages, with seats facing the stream. In the **churchyard** at the other end is the grave of Matthew Grimes. Described on his headstone as 'an old soldier', he fought at Waterloo and was afterwards a guard and then coffin-bearer of Napoleon on St Helena. The village **bridge** was reputedly built after Helmsley's Lord Feversham complained of water seeping into his carriage while crossing the still-adjacent ford.

Cyclists take a break

The slow way around Thornton

A pleasant 1½-mile (2.5-km) stroll is to the hamlet of **Ellerburn**. A caretaker of its 11th-century church once used the pulpit as a nesting box for a broody hen. The considerate priest preached from the lectern until the chicks were hatched.

In the church at **Brompton**, further along the A170, William Wordsworth married Mary Hutchinson on October 4, 1802. A copy of the marriage certificate is in the ★ **Wordsworth Gallery** (daily except Christmas 10am–5pm). A converted barn at Mary's former farmhouse home, Gallows Hill, the gallery houses an exhibition that explains the Wordsworth link and a parallel connection with Coleridge, who married Mary's sister, Sara.

Wordsworth Gallery

A plaque on **Brompton Hall**, a special school by the main road, honours **aviation pioneer Sir George Cayley**. A so-called 'glider' built and flown in 1853 by Cayley, Brompton's squire, was essentially the world's first aeroplane. Only the lack of a suitable engine denied Cayley his place in the record books as achieving the first powered flight – 50 years before the Wright Brothers. On its short flight across Brompton Dale, Cayley's glider carried his coachman, who afterwards quit, saying: 'I was hired to drive, not fly'. A neglected genius, Cayley also invented caterpillar traction and the spoked wheel, introduced the allotment system, and conceived the ideas of the self-righting lifeboat and the safety curtain and raked seats in theatres. The Battle of Trafalgar would have been won with ease if the Admiralty hadn't spurned his finned missiles, forerunner of the modern shell, which could far outshoot the heaviest cannon.

37

A neglected genius remembered

At **West Ayton**, another A170 village, the shell of a fortified 14th-century manor house may be viewed from its surrounding field. Neighbouring **East Ayton**, immediately across the bridge, has an acclaimed ★ **honey farm** (*see page 67*).

Before the honey farm, the route takes a sideroad on the left to the Forge Valley and Hackness. Clad with its national-nature-reserve woods, the steep-sided ★★ **Forge Valley** is another striking legacy of the Ice Age. Finding its outlet to Scarborough blocked by a glacier from the North Sea, the river Derwent escaped by gouging this narrow valley and Kirkham Gorge, near Malton.

Forge Valley

The road runs by the river, which slides romantically at the foot of the deciduous woods, where birds such as nuthatch, great spotted woodpecker, spotted flycatcher, and willow warbler may be seen. A waymarked 1½-mile (2.5-km) trail explores the woods. Emerging from the woods, the road soon crosses an artificial channel – the **Scalby Cut**. Another enterprise of the redoubtable Cayley this was his solution to frequent flooding of the Vale of Pickering by the Derwent. Controlled by sluices, the Cut takes a proportion of the Derwent's flow on its preglacial line to the sea at Scalby, north of Scarborough.

The road enters **Hackness** alongside the lake of 18th-century Hackness Hall, home of Lord Derwent (not open

38

to the public). The fine ★ **11th-century church** contains a cross inscribed in memory of the abbess of the abbey that stood here AD680–869. Founded by Whitby's St Hilda as a daughter abbey to her own, Hackness abbey provides the first-known reference to a church bell. Written c731, Bede's History tells how, on the night Hilda died, a Hackness nun dreamed she heard a bell, amid a vision of Hilda's soul ascending to heaven. This may have started the practice of tolling a bell at funerals.

A mile (1.6km) north of Hackness, on the Silpho road, **Reasty Bank** is a popular forest viewpoint. But the route goes to **Langdale End**, though those who don't wish to use the forest toll road may return to the A170 at Snainton by taking a left fork through Troutsdale. The signboard of the **Moorcock Inn** at Langdale End still displays the name Ada Martindale, who served her last pint in 1966. Little changed during her 40-year tenure, and not much more for the next 23, when the pub was run by her niece, Maud, the inn had no bar or draught beer, just a cosy front parlour, where Ada and Maud, like Ada's father as far back as 1901, served decanted bottled beer on trays. Though now in other hands and a bit more up to date, the inn nevertheless values its traditions, as the signboard shows.

About 4 miles (6.5km) beyond Langdale End, at Bickley, the route enters the 9-mile (14-km) ★ **Dalby Forest Drive** (open all year, summer toll £2.50). Planting of the 7,500-acre (3,000-hectare) Dalby Forest, the oldest in the Moors, began in 1921, just two years after the Forestry Commission was founded. The start of major felling in the 1970s ushered in a comprehensive 're-structuring' programme, to make the forest more scenic and appealing to wildlife. Straight lines have been abandoned and the proportion of deciduous trees has been increased. A **forest garden** at Bickley provides an introduction to the main species, which can be spotted on a 2½-mile (4-km) **habitat trail**, designed as a microcosm of the entire forest.

Amply-provided with parking places and picnic sites, the drive also passes Staindale Lake, where wildfowl can be observed from a shore path, accessible by wheelchair. The drive also gives access to the ★ **Bridestones** (National Trust, open all year, unrestricted). The result of uneven erosion, two groups of fantastically-weathered rocks, consisting of several strata of sandstones and limestones, dot the heather moor. Their name comes from an old Norse word meaning 'brink', a reference to their position between two steep little valleys.

Carefully retained at **Low Dalby**, where the drive ends, are towering Douglas firs from the original planting. More about the forest can be learned in a **Visitor Centre** (Easter to October daily 11am–4pm) before taking a minor road back to Thornton-le-Dale.

Route 7

Stokesley – Osmotherley – Snilesworth – Mount Grace Priory (46 miles/74km) *See map, pages 14–15*

A wealth of history and wide scenic variety characterise this route linking the Cleveland Hills and Hambleton Hills.

With the dramatic northern escarpment of the Cleveland Hills as its backdrop, ★ **Stokesley** is a particularly pleasing Georgian market town. Lining its wide, mainly-cobbled High Street, its three-storey buildings of mellow brick give it a vaguely Dutch appearance. The resemblance is strengthened by Levenside, a tranquil area behind the High Street and across the river Leven, linked by four footbridges, a medieval pack-horse bridge, and an iron road bridge. Handyside House, on the tree-lined West Green, is the official residence of the Bishop of Whitby. Each September Stokesley stages one of the largest one-day agricultural shows in the North of England. Its associated fair fills the High Street for most of the week.

Stokesley's tranquil Levenside

39

Leaving on the A172 Thirsk road, turn off for ★ **Carlton**. Graced by fine trees, the village cherishes the memory of a notable vicar, Canon John Latimer Kyle. When he arrived in 1894, the parish church, built only three years previously, had been mysteriously burned down, with the vicar accused of arson. Kyle's inspired leadership was crucial in achieving the completion of the present beautiful church, designed in 14th-century style by the eminent church architect Temple Moore. Believing inns to be as much part of village life as the church, Kyle took over the Fox and Hounds. An ardent fox-hunter and farmer, he announced hunt meets from the pulpit and laced his sermons with farming analogies. At his funeral in 1943, a wreath bore the message: 'From his hedges and ditches'. The Fox and Hounds closed in 1969.

From Carlton, drive to Faceby and rejoin the A172. At the next left, turn to enter Swainby and take a lane by the church. Climbing a short hill, this reaches ★ **Whorlton** – an atmospheric spot. Forlorn amid ditches and embankments stand a castle gatehouse and a ruined Norman church – the sole reminders of Whorlton village. Originally a *burgus*, a settlement within a castle, it was probably abandoned gradually as Swainby grew up on the more convenient plain.

Built in the 11th century, the castle entertained Edward II on a hunting trip in 1323. His hostess was a much-wooed heiress, Lucia de Thweng, who left her husband at Danby Castle to move in at Whorlton. At one time or another Lucia lived with almost every nobleman between

Whorlton castle

Whorlton church

Whorlton and Whitby. The gatehouse dates from shortly after her time, when the castle was converted into a fortified house. Its walls bear the marks of cannon balls and musket fire inflicted when it was besieged as a Royalist stronghold in the Civil War (1642–6).

The ★ **old church** served Swainby until 1875. Its avenue of yews sets the melancholy tone deepened by its roofless Norman nave. A peephole into the intact chancel reveals the canopied effigy of a knight, probably Sir Nicholas Meynell, a High Sheriff of Yorkshire in the 14th century. Still used occasionally, the church has a rare **mass dial** – seven holes on the outside south wall. Each day the priest placed a stick in a hole, the last hole signalling Mass to his illiterate flock.

The start of the Lyke Wake Walk

Returning to Swainby, take the Osmotherley road. Its steep section adopts a channel, Scarth Nick, scoured by the waters of a melting glacier. This was also part of the historic **Hambleton Drove Road**, along which sheep and cattle were driven on their way to markets in London. An unmetalled section strikes up the moor at Sheepwash, a popular picnic place in the cup of the Nick. An inscribed stone at **Sheepwash** marks the start of the **Lyke Wake Walk**. Finishing at Ravenscar (*see page 58*) this 42-mile (68-km) trek across the moors, keeping as much as possible to the highest ground, was devised in 1955 by local farmer Bill Cowley (1915–94). Its name stems from Cleveland's ancient Lyke Wake Dirge, which appears in the *Oxford Book of English Verse*. *Lyke* is an old Norse word for a corpse, over which a *wake*, or watch was kept. In the dirge, the dead person's soul undergoes a terrible journey across a fearful moor. Bill Cowley was reminded of this as he and a handful of supporters struggled to make the crossing over the then largely trackless moors. Despite its coffin emblem, the walk does not follow old corpse roads, none of which exists in the moors.

By the mid 1970s, about 20,000 people a year were tackling the walk, which must be completed within 24 hours to earn membership of the Lyke Wake Club. The severe erosion this caused led to sustained publicity aimed at discouraging large sponsored groups. The annual number of 'crossings' is now an acceptable 3,000. As a homage to the heather moorland the walk, though now paved in parts, remains a classic.

Passing Cod Beck reservoir (*cod* here comes from the Celtic *coed*, meaning woody), the route reaches ★★ **Osmotherley**. 'Ossy', as the village is known, is hoisted on a shared shoulder of the Cleveland and Hambleton Hills, with pubs and shops grouped at a crossroads with a market cross. The place is full of sturdy moorland character.

Osmotherley in bloom

John Wesley (1703–91) preached here 16 times. He at first stood on the so-called **barter table**, a stone slab on stumpy legs by the market cross, from which dairy produce was once sold. When the Methodists built their cottage-like chapel in 1744, up the passage that now brings the Cleveland Way into the village, he used a stool, still kept there. He also preached in the house of an ex Roman Catholic priest, defrocked for marrying his housekeeper. The priest's former home, the **Old Hall**, in the main street, is today occupied by monks from Ampleforth.

Wesley's barter table

On a grassy shelf off Rueberry Lane is the Roman Catholic shrine of the ★ **Lady Chapel** (open all year). Almost certainly in existence well before it was licensed for Mass in 1397, this former hermitage might well be what drew the Carthusian monks who founded nearby Mount Grace Priory (*see page 42*). A place of secret pilgrimage when Catholics were persecuted in the 17th century, the chapel eventually fell into ruin but was restored in 1960 by the Roman Catholic Church. The Ampleforth Benedictines celebrate Evensong there each Saturday afternoon.

Osmotherley was once a linen-weaving centre. Its Youth Hostel was a mill, and the church porch bears deep grooves where weavers sharpened their shuttles. The engraved **outline of a clog** on a South End cottage is the original sign of one of several clogmakers in the village.

41

Leave Osmotherley and drive to Hawnby. The road soon passes the farmhouse and tearoom of ★★ **Chequers**, a former drovers' pub. Still displayed is its teasing sign: *Be not in haste, step in and taste. Ale tomorrow – for nothing.* (*See page 69*). Beyond Chequers, a path leads up a nab to the finest stretch of the Drove Road, a green lane along the edge of the 1,100-ft (400-m) Black Hambleton. A highlight of the Cleveland Way, this was the favourite walk of author-vet James Herriot.

Tea at Chequers

Arden Hall

A stirring drive across lonely **Snilesworth Moors** culminates in an abrupt change in the landscape. With the wild moor at its back, the village of **Hawnby**, on the sunny south slope of its eponymous hill, gazes across a sheltered bowl of verdant woods and pastures. Well worth the 3-mile (5-km) detour, up the dead-end Kepwick road is an intimate view of ★ **Arden Hall**, a particularly lovely Queen Anne (early 18th-century) house, home of the Earl and Countess of Mexborough. Its great billowing yew hedge may have been planted by the nuns of a nunnery that stood here from c1150 to 1536. Fragments of the building are incorporated in the house.

From Hawnby take the Helmsley road, but where it turns left – up the hill beyond the bridge – go straight on. Crossing the Drove Road, the route descends to **Boltby**, an unspoilt village of particularly warm-looking sandstone, and thence to **Felixkirk**, in whose parish church, noted for its fine 14th-century effigies, the funeral service of James Herriot took place in 1994. He lived in the nearby hamlet of Thirlby.

42

Over Silton's Norman church

Meandering byroads take the route through the quiet villages of Kirby Knowle, Cowesby, Kepwick, Nether Silton and Over Silton. A monument at **Kepwick**, a neat estate village, commemorates squire John Boyer, who died in 1891. Isolated in a field at **Over Silton** is a simple little ★ **Norman church**. In 1995, worshippers rejected a £10,000 bequest to install electricity. One of them observed: 'The soft candlelight on the old stonework creates a feeling of centuries of worship'.

Mount Grace Priory

From Over Silton take the Northallerton road to the A19; turn right on the dual carriageway. Signposted off this after a short distance is ★★★ **Mount Grace Priory** (National Trust/ English Heritage, April to September daily 10am–6pm, October daily and November to March Wednesday to Sunday 10am–4pm).

The best-preserved of England's nine medieval Carthusian monasteries, Mount Grace is probably Britain's most distinctive monastic ruin. Carthusian personal seclusion demanded a wholly different pattern to the abbeys of other orders. The church is no bigger than many parish churches, but the cloister, around which the 20 or so monks lived in individual cells, is the largest in England. In reality a well-appointed house, superior to most in Britain until this century, each cell had piped water, a study, living room with fire, workroom, and herb garden. Food was served through an L-shaped hatch, denying server and receiver sight of each other. A cell has been restored, and an excellent exhibition is housed in a handsome Jacobean mansion, converted from the priory's guesthouse.

Return to Stokesley on the A19 and A172.

Route 8

Great Ayton – Esk Valley – Whitby (31 miles/50km)
See map, pages 14–15

A string of villages by the beautiful Esk, Yorkshire's only salmon river, provides rich interest as this route links the place of Captain Cook's boyhood with Whitby, where his great seagoing career began.

Grown in recent years but still penetrated by green fields, **Great Ayton** is one of Yorkshire's best known villages. Two greens, High and Low, are almost linked by the river Leven, which flows through the village for half a mile. Shoppers are treated to a waterfall where the river tumbles over a weir. Benignly looking down on the village is the 'mini-Matterhorn' of Roseberry Topping, one of Yorkshire's most popular hills.

Great Ayton

Born in 1728 at Marton, now absorbed into Middlesbrough, James Cook spent the years 1735–45 at Great Ayton, where his father was bailiff, or farm manager, at Airyholme Farm, on the slope of Roseberry Topping. Cook's schoolroom, in the village centre, is now a small ★ **museum** (April to October daily 2–4.30pm, also weekday mornings in August). With Cook's reputed desk and his portable inkwell as prized exhibits, the museum presents informative displays on Cook's voyages and 18th-century Great Ayton.

43

Local hero

The family worshipped at the Norman **All Saints Church**, where Cook's mother and five of his seven brothers and sisters are buried. Nearby, on Easby Lane, an obelisk marks the site of the cottage, built by Cook's father, to which the explorer's parents retired in 1755. Though Great Ayton now bitterly regrets the shipment of the cottage to Melbourne, Australia, in 1934, few protested at the time.

After the obligatory tasting of a Suggitt's ice cream (*see page 67*), leave Great Ayton by Station Road. At the first junction, just beyond the Quaker-founded Ayton School, stands Britain's only remaining Victorian **cast iron urinal** that is still in use.

Roseberry Topping

Beyond the station a public track on the left goes to Airyholm Farm, still a working farm, and the 1,051-ft (320-m) ★★ **Roseberry Topping**. To the Vikings it was Odin's Hill, and an old verse says: *If Roseberry Topping wears a cap, let Cleveland then beware of clap.*

Where the road reaches open moor, a path on the right leads in 10 minutes to ★ **Captain Cook's Monument** on Easby Hill. Erected in 1827 this commands a fine view of the main switchback ridge of the Cleveland Hills.

Botton Community member

Walker at Danby

44

View from Danby Beacon

On reaching Kildale, turn for Commondale but soon take the Westerdale road, with its glorious view (*see page 23*). Turn off for Castleton, crossing the infant Esk at Dibble Bridge – with big beeches and a lovely house.

Beyond Castleton, the unpretentious northern capital of Eskdale, a signpost directs to **Botton Hall**. Since 1955 this Edwardian country house, built for a member of the Macmillan publishing family, has been the administrative hub of the ★ **Botton Community**. Divided into 'family' groups on six farms at the head of Danby Dale, about 170 mentally handicapped people, in partnership with 120 or so 'co-workers', live a largely self-sufficient life. Run by the Camphill Village Trust, this was, and is, the world's largest working community for mentally handicapped people. Its social focus is a village square, with Post Office, bookshop, coffee shop and gift shop. Visitors are welcome, and an open day is held each July.

Buried at the isolated **Danby church**, which was central for the scattered farms before 'modern' Danby evolved near the railway station, is Canon John Atkinson. Vicar from 1847 to 1900, his book *Forty Years in a Moorland Parish* is a regional classic.

From Castleton or Botton drive to Danby (*see page 27*). Continue towards Lealholm, but at the Moors Centre (*see page 27*) go straight up the hill. A left fork goes to ★ **Danby Beacon**. Site of a Napoleonic beacon and World War II radar station, this commands the most extensive view within the national park.

Returning to the road from the Moors Centre, turn left. On reaching a 'T' junction, turn right for Lealholm. A **roadside stone** on the left commemorates the two crewmen of a US fighter bomber that crashed here in 1979. The villagers are convinced that the pilot deliberately made

a change of course at the last second to avoid the village, where there were 55 children in the school.

From Lealholm (*see page 27*) continue to **Glaisdale**, whose stone terraces accommodated workers at an iron-works active 1863–9. Spanning the Esk at the foot of the hills is a graceful high-arched packhorse bridge. Known as the ★★ **Beggar's Bridge**, it gets its name from a ro-mantic legend of the courtship of the squire's daughter by local farmhand Thomas Ferris. Told by the squire that his daughter wasn't going to marry 'a beggar', Tom vowed to make his fortune. The night before he sailed from Whitby on this mission, a flood on the Esk, at that time crossed only by a ford or stepping stones, prevented him bidding farewell to his sweetheart. Eventually returning rich – the fruit of piracy some say – he not only married the girl but built a bridge for future lovers. There is almost certainly some truth in the tale, for a 17th-century Hull shipowner, Thomas Ferries, left substantial bequests to Glaisdale parish church, and his initials, with the date 1619, are on the outer upstream parapet of the bridge.

Beggar's Bridge at Glaisdale

*Egton Bridge
stepping stones*

45

From the bridge, a path through ★ **Arncliffe Woods**, part of the Coast to Coast Walk, makes a pleasant 1½-mile (2.5-km) ramble to ★ **Egton Bridge**, which has a double set of stepping stones where the Esk divides round a wooded island. They are reached down a path by a tall old mill, with broken weir. The path emerges near the attrac-tive Horseshoe Hotel. As its datestone testifies, the beau-tiful **sandstone bridge** was built only in 1993. It replaced an ugly iron bridge erected in 1930 when the original 16th-century structure was washed away. The latest bridge is a perfect copy of the 16th-century version, but on stronger foundations. It's a pity a similar bridge couldn't have been built next to the Beggar's Bridge, where another clumsy iron bridge has been replaced by one of no greater beauty.

Containing some fine murals of Biblical scenes, ★ **St Hedda's Roman Catholic Church** (1866–7) also has a shrine to a martyred priest, Nicholas Postgate. Caught bap-tising a baby at the age of 80, he was hanged, drawn and quartered at York in 1679. The shrine's relics, which in-clude his prayer book and sacraments' box, were found 150 years after his death in a secret room in a house by the parish church, in which he celebrated Mass.

Frescoes in St Hedda's

In August, St Hedda's schoolroom is the venue for the ★★ **Egton Bridge Old Gooseberry Show** (*see page 65*) Between 1952 and 1982 the record for the world's biggest gooseberry was held by a near-2-oz (56-gram) specimen, grown at Postgate's Mass House, up the bank.

The villages of Grosmont (*see page 35*), Sleights, which has a fish pass for the salmon, and Ruswarp, with boat-ing on the Esk, complete the route, which finishes in Whitby (*see page 46*).

Whitby harbour

The crow's nest

The swing bridge

Victorian jet-workers

Route 9

Whitby Walkabout (1½-miles/2.4km) *See map, page 47*

Fondly known to locals as 't'awd spot', Whitby enters history with the Saxon Abbey founded by St Hilda in 657. But it was not until the Dissolution of the later Norman abbey in 1539 that the modest settlement at the mouth of the Esk, the only safe haven along 100 miles (160km) of coast, began significantly to grow. In the 18th century its thriving trade in coal and alum made it the 7th most important port in the United Kingdom. Boosted by shipbuilding and whaling, its expansion produced the celebrated townscape, a magical jumble of pantiled cottages climbing from the harbour. By the time Whitby became a major centre for the manufacture of jet jewellery in Victorian days, it was already viewed as 'quaint' – the quality that sustains its main industry today, tourism.

Start at the Information Centre on New Quay Road. The **mock crow's nest** ❶ commemorates whaling skippers William Scoresby Senior and Junior, the elder of whom devised this look-out. Designed by George Andrews, the nearby **railway station** ❷ was built when the Whitby–Pickering Railway was extended in 1847. Its original terminus was further up the harbour, on reclaimed land where Captain Cook's ships were built. The opening of the line was celebrated with a feast at the **Angel Hotel** ❸. Ironically, the Angel was the centre of Whitby's coaching trade, killed by the railway. Introduced in 1788, a coach to Leeds, 65 miles away, took 10½ hours.

Round the corner, the ★★ **swing bridge** ❹ is a key element, physically and visually, in the Whitby scene. While separating the upper and lower harbours, it holds together the two sides of the town, East and West, like the clasp of a fine old necklace. The fifth bridge on or near this site, it was opened in 1909 and is Britain's only swing bridge with two moveable leaves.

Crossing the bridge to the East Side, turn left into Sandgate. A former haunt of smugglers, this leads to the cobbled and paved **Market Place** ❺. Dairy produce was sold in the open part of the elegant **Town Hall**, designed by Jonathan Pickernell in 1788. The upper room, where the council met, now displays local craft goods. Off the Market Place, the stumpy **Fish Pier** ❻, built c1691, was the fish quay until the west side of the harbour was developed. Whitby's lifeboat is now moored there.

From the Town Hall turn left into Church Street. At its sharp bend, the ★ **Victorian Jet Works** ❼ (all year daily from 9.30am) is an authentic jet workshop, transferred from an inconvenient building up a yard. In 1870, when the craze for jet reached its height, following the adoption of jet jewellery by Queen Victoria in mourning for Prince Albert, more than 200 jet workshops, with over 1,500 workers, were operating in Whitby. Most of their jet, a fossilised wood similar to coal, but much older and harder, came from the Cleveland Hills. A small amount of jewellery is still made, and a jet carver can sometimes be seen in the Jet Works.

Jet carver in action today

Tate Hill, a narrow lane by the Jet Works, leads to ★ **Tate Hill Pier** ❽. Originally called the Burgess Pier, because Whitby's burgesses, or leading citizens, paid for its erection c1545, this was Whitby's first pier. An inscribed slab records its role as the home of Whitby's lifeboats between 1822–63. Rebuilt in 1766, it features in Bram Stoker's *Dracula* (1897) as the place where the Count, in the form of 'an immense black dog', leaps ashore when his schooner is wrecked in Whitby harbour.

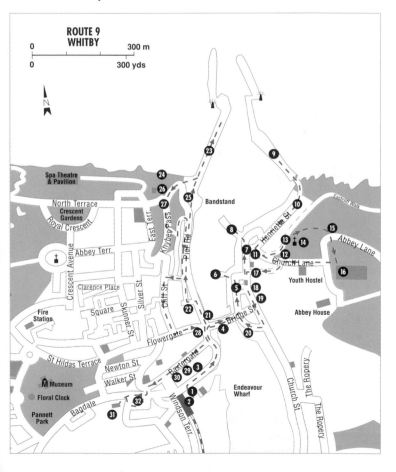

Fortune's kipper house

From the pier, climb Tate Hill's left fork and turn left into **Henrietta Street**. This was once Whitby's most desirable street, but the merchants and shipbuilders moved out following a large landslip in 1787. Landslip still troubles the street, and its far end, which gives access to the **East Pier 9** is sometimes sealed off.

Built c1657, the East Pier was reconstructed in its present form in 1844–50. Spanned by a footbridge, the gap between pier and cliff was left as a cartway for alum works at Saltwick. Henrietta Street is home to ★★ **Fortune's kipper house 10** (*see page 67*).

(*see page 67*)

Church Stairs

48

Return to Henrietta Street's junction with Church Street. In the wall of the facing cottage are **ammonite fossils 11**. Common in the cliffs, these are fancifully said to have been snakes. Infesting the Saxon abbey, they were turned into stone by St Hilda. Now climb the ★★★ **Church Stairs 12**, a flight of broad stone steps at the head of Church Street. As their name indicates these serve the church, not the abbey as many assume. The seats at intervals were coffin rests! First mentioned in 1370, the steps were wooden until the late 18th century. Tradition demands that visitors count the steps, returning to the bottom if they miscount. The correct number, engraved at the top, is 199.

With the red-roofed town directly below, the ★★★ **view from the clifftop** reveals Whitby's isolated position – 'between the heather and the Northern Sea', as local author Mary Linskill described it in the title of a novel. An **ornate cross 13** commemorates Caedmon, the cowherd poet (*see page 64*), while beyond, in its windswept graveyard crowded with weathered headstones, stands the marvellous ★★★ **St Mary's parish church 14**. Described by Sir Nikolaus Pevsner as 'hard to believe, impossible not to love', St Mary's is undoubtedly among the half dozen most

St Mary's parish church

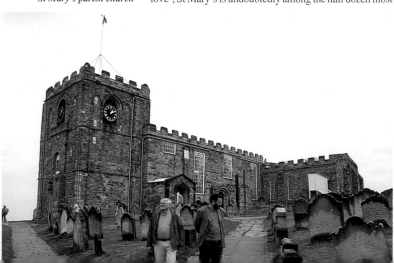

fascinating churches in England. Inserted in its Norman walls are large clear-glass Georgian domestic windows of Gothic design. More windows up in the roof evoke a ship's cabin, and a maze of box pews and galleries enables the still-candlelit church to seat almost 2,000. Raised on barley-sugar columns and with a separate outside entrance, a pompous squire's pew obscures the Norman chancel arch, and fixed to a three-decker pulpit is the ear-trumpet by which the deaf wife of a former incumbent was required to listen to his sermons.

Huntrodds memorial

Built into the wall outside is a touching **★★ memorial to Francis and Mary Huntrodds**. Born on the same day in 1600, they got married on their birthday. They also died on their birthday, aged 80, within hours of each other. A verse says: *So fit a match surely could never be, both in their lives and in their deaths agree.*

Beyond the church, Abbey Plain is the site of Hilda's abbey (657–867). In 664 it hosted the Synod of Whitby, which agreed the method of calculating Easter. Erected much later, a **medieval cross** ⓯ perhaps tells of a community up here, alongside the early Norman abbey and with a market place focused on the cross, before the harbourside was colonised. This would explain the peculiar clifftop location of the parish church.

49

The medieval cross

Gaunt and defiant, the ruins of the **★ Norman abbey** ⓰ founded in 1078 (English Heritage, April to September daily 10am–6pm, October to March daily 10am–4pm) are chiefly the shell of its 13th- and 14th-century church. This stands over 100 yards (90m) long, with a spectacular rose window. On December 16, 1914, bits were blasted off the west front by a pair of German cruisers that bombarded the town. Adjoining the abbey, another roofless shell is the remains of a late 17th-century manorial banqueting hall. Destroyed by a gale in the late 18th century, it is to become a new Abbey Visitors Centre.

Whitby Abbey

From the abbey go down the cobbled **Church Lane**, alongside the 199 steps, which the lane probably predates. Directly below the first house, take the footway fronting Abbey Terrace East, from where steps descend to **★ Blackburn's Yard** ⓱. An attractive example of the 100 or so yards that still exist in Whitby, this was the birthplace, in a since-demolished cottage whose site is marked by a tablet, of Mary Linskill (1840–91), a novelist once compared to George Eliot. Her father was constable of a lockup at the bottom of the yard.

Blackburn's Yard

Re-entering Church Street, turn left. Beyond the Market Place, **Black Horse Yard** ⓲ was the midden of Hilda's abbey. Unearthed from the midden and now in Whitby Museum (*see page 51*) are items including a bone comb with a religious inscription and a 7th-century lead

Captain Cook and his pub

Bustling West Pier

Lifeboat heritage

seal from Rome, perhaps handled by Hilda herself. The **White Horse and Griffin** ⑲, with its elegant doorcase, was visited by both Captain Cook and Charles Dickens. Cook is said to have met shipbuilders here to discuss the conversion of the Whitby colliers for his voyages. Dickens dined there in 1844, later observing that 'oyster-shell grottos were the only view from the best private room'.

Reaching Bridge Street, go straight on then turn right into **Grape Lane**. Overlooking the harbour is the ship owner's home where young James Cook lodged as an apprentice 1746–9. Now the ★ **Captain Cook Memorial Museum** ⑳ (late March to early November daily 9.45am–5pm, other March weekends 11am–3pm), this is furnished as in Cook's time and contains much material relating to his voyages. A potent link with Cook is the unchanged attic, where he and the other apprentices bedded down on straw mattresses.

Re-crossing the bridge, turn right and follow St Ann's Staith, Marine Parade, and Pier Road to the West Pier. Until major harbour works of the late 18th and 19th century, this entire area was within the harbour. In **St Ann's Staith** ㉑, houses on stilts stood over the water. Until Marine Parade was built, a ★ **magnificent mid-18th century house** ㉒ in Haggersgate – on the left where St Ann's Staith joins the parade – enjoyed open views down the harbour. It was built for whaler John Yeoman.

Effectively opening up Whitby's west side, which soon claimed the fishing trade, the new quayside was the logical follow-up to a complete rebuild of the ★★ **West Pier** ㉓, constructed on its present line in 1734–50, with work continuing until 1814. Its huge blocks of stone were hauled by oxen from a quarry at Aislaby, Eskdale, which later supplied similar blocks for the East Pier. Capstans, several of which survive, winched-in sailing ships, and guns were mounted at the pier's bull-nosed end and on a crescent-shaped battery at its foot. Now **Battery Parade** ㉔, this still has its turreted powder stores and guardhouse, the latter a café. Designed by Francis Pickernell, grandson of Jonathan (*see page 46*), the fluted West Pier lighthouse was erected in 1831, followed by its plainer East Pier counterpart in 1854. But vessels approaching Whitby harbour at the angle necessary to stay in deep water continued to overshoot and end on Saltwick rocks. To reduce this hazard, the distinctive pier extensions, with their plank decks on wooden pillars, were built in 1909–14. Housed in the ★ **Lifeboat Museum** ㉕ near the pier is Britain's last rowing lifeboat. It was used as a back-up at Whitby until 1957.

From the pier, turn up the hill called Khyber Pass. Steps lead to a fine **bronze statue of Captain Cook** ㉖, gazing out to sea. Views of the abbey and church are framed by a **whalebone arch** ㉗, with a plaque giving details of the whaling industry (1753–1837). Across the road, **East Terrace** is linked to Lewis Carroll (*see page 64*), while further along the clifftop, **No 6 Royal Crescent** is where Bram Stoker stayed while writing chapters of *Dracula*. The development of this area was due to 'Railway King' George Hudson, who bought Whitby West Fields in 1845 to establish Whitby as a resort.

The whalebone arch

Crossing the public garden in front of East Terrace, go through a tunnel off Khyber Pass. Steps twist down to a footway behind cottages and the amusement arcades. Until Pier Road was constructed this was the way to the town. Turn right on the footway and right again where it ends to climb paved Pier Lane. On reaching Cliff Street, with pleasant town houses, turn left. Passing open-fronted **McLacklin's Yard** on the right, enter the shopping street of Flowergate. Go to the bottom where ★★ **The Sutcliffe Gallery** ㉘ exhibits – and sells – the evocative Victorian photographs of Whitby and its hinterland by Frank Sutcliffe (1853–1941).

The Sutcliffe Gallery

By the gallery, the footway of Golden Lion Bank leads to **Old Market Place**, setting of the market until 1640. From there turn right into Baxtergate, the main shopping street. Up worn steps behind iron railings, a **dignified house** c1700 ㉙, now a solicitor's office, was home of Whitby's first shipbuilder, Jarvis Coates. Shipyard workers celebrated launches in the ★ **Old Ship Launch** ㉚, now the Old Smuggler, a snug inglenook café. The ship's figurehead on its wall is said to be from a smuggler's ship captured by Excisemen, who erected it as a warning to other smugglers, who also patronised the inn.

Continue to the end of Baxtergate at Victoria Square. Diagonally opposite, the 16th-century **Bagdale Hall** ㉛, now a hotel, might be Whitby's oldest house. When it was built it was described as being 'nere unto Whitbie', with fields still separating it from the harbour. Stepping stones crossed a beck that wasn't culverted until 1866. Returning along Baxtergate, go down the second passage on the right to enter ★★ **Linskill Square** ㉜. Named after an alum manufacturer, this is Whitby's best preserved yard. From its well-kept cottages owners no longer throw rubbish into the central drainage channel, a serious health hazard in Victorian days. A passage at the far end emerges on to Station Square, close to the walk's start.

Bagdale Hall

Whitby's rich history is absorbingly represented in the ★★ **Whitby Museum** in Pannet Park (May to September Monday to Saturday 9.30am–5.30pm, Sunday 2pm–5.30pm, October to April daily, for times tel: 01947 602908). Old Whitby in pictures is the theme of ★ **Whitby Pictorial Archives**, Grape Lane (daily 10.30am–4.30pm).

Bird's eye view of Staithes

Route 10

A lifetime by the sea

Whitby – Runswick Bay – Staithes (22 miles/35km) *See map, pages 14–15*

NOTE: Whitby is the natural centre for exploring the coast. The A174/A171 'Coast Road', though handy for visiting the trio of Cornish-style villages described in the following two routes, reveals little of the magnificence of the coastline itself. A mixture of rocky coves and wide bays, defended by bold headlands pounded by the often savage North Sea, this can be explored properly only on foot. The well-maintained coast path makes this easy, and south of Whitby, the parallel footpath on the former coastal railway enables a wide variety of circular walks to be devised. Particularly good are the walks between Staithes and Runswick Bay, Sandsend or Kettleness and Runswick Bay (in that direction), and Whitby to Robin Hood's Bay.

Heading north from Whitby, Route 10 discovers the inspiration of Captain Cook.

Shelter at Sandsend

From Whitby (*see page 46*) take the A174 to Sandsend. Known locally as the Maharajah's road, most of this stretch of the A174 was built as a toll road by the Maharajah Duleep Singh. Dispossessed of his Punjab kingdom by Queen Victoria, he leased nearby Mulgrave Castle between 1859 and 1863. An unfounded legend is that the road, which replaced a longer inland route or the beach, was built because the Maharajah's elephants didn't like getting sand between their toes. Alas, elephants were never actually kept at the castle.

The **roadside cottage** facing the golf links was the road's toll house. Ahead, across the bay, is a good view of ★ **Sandsend**. The bare headland is the result of the extraction and processing of alum, which took place there from 1615 to 1867 – the longest-lasting industrial operation in the Moors. Remains can be seen from the trackbed-footpath of the former coastal railway, accessible from a car park at the foot of Lythe Bank.

From Sandsend's other (East Row) car park, walks lead to **Mulgrave Woods** (Wednesday and weekends, by permission of Lord Normanby). Clothing two steep valleys, these are particularly attractive when snowdrops and bluebells picturesquely carpet the mound of a ruined **Norman Castle**. Not open to the public, the ruin preceded the present Mulgrave Castle, home of Lord Normanby, the core of which was built c1735 for a daughter of James II.

Seaside rain or shine

The route continues up the 1-in-4 Lythe Bank and keeps with the A174 until the signposted road to ★★ **Runswick Bay**. Although there is a car park in the village, the best way to enter Runswick is on foot. The short path starting by the Cliffemount Hotel is the original road. Abandoned in 1961 because of landslip, this leads straight into the maze of pretty cottages. On their south-facing cliff, most enjoy a view of the often Mediterranean-looking bay, enclosed by a headland at Kettleness.

The minimal fishing still carried out is of the leisure variety, but in mid-Victorian days about 40 boats supported a population of about 500. Today, fewer than a dozen of the village's 92 cottages are permanent homes. The car park occupies the site of herring-curing houses.

Aspects of Runswick

Ready for service in the tractor house of the lifeboat station is **one of Britain's few independent lifeboats**. The RNLI closed its Runswick station in 1978, but local people and yachtsmen, convinced there was still a need, raised cash to buy and run the community's own inshore rescue craft. Fully recognised by the Coastguard Service, which co-ordinates rescues, the present boat is the third since the first was launched in 1982. Details of the 70-odd missions are recorded on boards in the Royal Hotel. Honoured by his **photograph in the village chapel** is lifeboatman Robert Patton. Cox of the village's first motor lifeboat, in 1934 he selflessly gave up a chance to avoid being crushed between the lifeboat and a wallowing steamship while plucking a seaman to safety. Later dying from his injuries, he was posthumously awarded the RNLI's gold medal.

The landslip that destroyed the road was merely one of many. For though Runswick has a sea wall, its erosion problems stem mainly from a buildup of rainwater in the heavy boulder clay, which occasionally breaks away. One night in 1682 the entire village, apart from one house, fell into the sea. Luckily, the early tremors were felt by a party returning from a funeral wake. By rousing the other villagers they prevented loss of life.

'Wrecking' – plundering ships that came to grief in the bay – was once such a Runswick industry that children were taught to pray: 'God bless Ma and Pa, and send us a good wreck by morning'. Like their moorland neighbours, Runswick folk also believed in 'hobs' – hobgoblins. A hob credited with the power to cure whooping cough lived in one of the caves marked on the map as Hob Holes – at the end of the bay. Mothers carried their sick infants there and called out: 'Ma bairn's gotten t'kink cough. Tak't off, tak't off'. The success rate is not recorded.

From Runswick, return to the A174 at Hinderwell. A lane at the far end leads to **Port Mulgrave**. Paddle steamers operated out of this small harbour, built in 1857 to ferry iron ore from nearby mines to blast furnaces on Tyneside. But though several rows of cottages survive, very little is left of the harbour, which shipped its last ore in 1921.

Staithes

54

First sight of neighbouring ★★★ **Staithes** is not very promising – a raggle-taggle of housing estates, bungalows, and terraces of ironstone-mine cottages. But directly beyond its Bank Top, where cars must be parked, the road plunges steeply to reveal the old village – a world of screaming gulls swooping over cottages crammed into a crevice in the cliffs. From Bank Foot, the cobbled street makes two sharp bends before emerging at the harbour, overlooked by two sheer nabs. There is great drama in all this. Rugged, even a shade dour, Staithes is a place of powerful atmosphere.

A paradise for gulls

When first noted, in 1451, Staithes was probably only a landing place for a since-vanished settlement a mile inland. But from the 16th century it became one of Britain's most renowned shellfishing villages. The industry peaked in 1885 when around 300 fishermen manned 120 boats. Though only four or five boats operate full-time today, these maintain an unbroken tradition of full-time fishing spanning more than five centuries. Crabs and lobsters are still the main summer catch. In winter they are replaced by codling, caught on lines.

Boats are moored in the beck

A beck divides Staithes into two. **Cowbar** is the official name of the cottages on the far side. With their own road access, these are even in a different local authority area to Staithes proper. The beck is the safe – and photogenic – mooring of the Staithes boats, small inshore craft. On the Cowbar side stands the chapel-like lifeboat house, opened in 1875. Today, as often in the past, Staithes and Runswick share an RNLI boat, whose story is told in a booklet available at the lifeboat house. The road slanting up from the footbridge leads to a much-photographed ★★ **bird's eye view** of the incredibly huddled village.

Staithes bonnets

Since its last two regular wearers died in 1995, the **Staithes bonnet**, a famous sight, has all but vanished from the streets. It is worn in the post office, where the proprietor's wife and her assistant have adopted it to meet hygiene regulations covering the sale of cooked meats. This perpetuates the bonnet's role as working headgear, for its original purpose was to protect the women's hair as they carried lines and baskets on their heads. With its quilted brim and flared neckpiece the bonnet still appears en masse on Lifeboat Day, in July, and souvenir bonnets can be bought in the general store opposite the post office.

The High Street's final bend takes it round the **Cod and Lobster Inn**. Jutting into the harbour this has been virtually destroyed by the sea at least five times, most recently in 1953. In 1830 the waves also claimed the shop where, in 1745–6, 17-year-old James Cook served as assistant to grocer and draper William Sanderson. Brought up in Great Ayton, (*see page 43*), Cook first felt the pull of the sea at Staithes. Within 18 months he was apprenticed to Whitby shipowner John Walker (*see page 50*), and the rest, as they say, is history.

Wreck at the Heritage Centre

The double-fronted harbourside house now known as **Cook's Cottage** became the new premises of the business that was destroyed in the 1830 storm. A wealth of material on Cook and other facets of Staithes' history is in the ★ **Staithes Heritage Centre** (March to December daily, January to February weekends 10am–5pm), in a converted High Street chapel.

From the harbourside, an adventurous return to the car park begins at the 18-inch (40-cm) wide passageway of Dog Loup, a few yards above the Cook cottage. After squeezing through the passage, simply keep climbing between the cottages. From a knoll at the top, by a white cottage, is another ★ **fine view of the harbour**. There is a good view of the village's two breakwaters, built in 1928.

Rearing up northwards, the 700-ft (213-m) **Boulby Cliff** is the highest point on England's eastern seaboard and the second highest around the entire coast. Opened in the teeth of fierce opposition in 1973, the nearby Boulby Potash Mine is the only one of its kind in Britain. From the foot of its 3,750-ft (1,143-m) main shaft, the deepest in Europe, miners travel to the seams in Ford Transit vans. A by-product of the mine, which employs 960 people, is rock salt for gritting roads.

If returning to Whitby, the A174 is recommended for the ★ **panoramic view** across the bay from Lythe Bank. Alternatively, take the Dalehouse road opposite Staithes lane end. In Dalehouse turn right along the pretty, narrow Ridge Lane, which joins the A171 Guisborough–Whitby moor road at Scaling Dam.

55

Calmer waters

Robin Hood's Bay

Route 11

Whitby – Robin Hood's Bay – Ravenscar – Whitby
(30 miles/48km) *See map, pages 14–15*

Where the countryside meets the coast

St Stephen's 'old church'

The most captivating of the coastal villages and an aborted seaside resort are the contrasting highlights of this dramatic drive, which can be extended to Scarborough.

From the A171 Scarborough road at High Hawsker, take the B1477 for Robin Hood's Bay. Soon, the finest ★★ **view** of countryside and coast in the national park opens up. Sweeping down from the higher ground, a great arc of fields and woods leads the eye across the bay to the majestic headland of Ravenscar's South Cheek. Towering some 657ft (188m) above the waves, the latter is the unlikely setting of the stillborn resort to be visited later.

Meanwhile, at the roadside 1 mile (0.6km) from Robin Hood's Bay is ★ **St Stephen's** 'old church', the former parish church (July to September Saturday afternoon). Built in 1821 this replaced a church of 1107 on the same spot. The plainness of the church, with its modest bellcote and clear-glass windows, is due to the strong influence of Methodism when it was built. This is also reflected inside, where the pulpit, midway along the south wall, was positioned to focus minds on The Word, rather than the rituals inherent in gazing at an altar. In their box pews, some worshippers sat with their backs to the altar. On display is a rare set of Maiden's Garlands. These coloured ribbons were carried by village girls at the funeral of a young virgin. The origin of the custom, recorded at only 11 places in Britain, all on the coast, is unknown.

In view from the churchyard is the tower of the 'new' St Stephen's. Located at the top of ★★★ **Robin Hood's**

Bay – known locally simply as 'Bay' – this was built in 1870 to a design by George Street, architect of the London Law Courts. Its stained glass includes a splendid scene of fishermen with nets. Fishing and farming, the two traditional strands of local life, are also depicted on an oak porch-screen made by Tom Whittaker of Littlebeck (1910–91), a noted furniture maker and woodcarver. His gnome trademark appears on several items in the church.

Ignored by most visitors, a number of good looking Victorian and Edwardian houses at Bank Top tell of a surprising facet of Bay's history. They were built for Bay shipowners when, in the final century of the sailing-ship era, many ocean-going vessels based at Whitby and other ports were owned by folk in this small fishing village: 174 in 1867, for instance. This shipowning activity seems even more odd when Bay's own 'Dock' is visited. The sudden end of the steep main street, this is merely a tiny square, with a cobbled slipway up which the sea surges at high tide. The few boats hauled up there are used mainly for casual fishing.

Off the main street run the snickets and narrow lanes that, together with the diminutive Dock, give Robin Hood's Bay its Toytown character. Time should be spent exploring this intimate network, full of odd corners and surprisingly sunny little squares, with rose-clad cottages. It takes several visits to get to know it.

57

On and off the main street

The link with Robin Hood is obscure. One tale says the fabled outlaw kept a boat in the bay as an ultimate means of escape. He perhaps knew the district through reputedly being drafted in by the Abbot of Whitby to repel those Danish invaders. The first record of 'Robbyn Huddes Bay' dates from 1538, when the traveller John Leland noted it as 'a fischar tounlet of 20 bootes'. Though Leland called Whitby a 'great fischar town', Bay subsequently overtook it. In 1816, when Whitby was preoccupied with whaling, alum and coal and had only nine fishermen, Bay had 130 – the largest number in Yorkshire. But its fishing industry petered out in the 1930s.

Probably its biggest industry was smuggling. By the slipway is a ★ **tunnel** that discharges King's Beck. Usually walkable for a short distance, this was the spine of a network of smaller tunnels, which could be entered from cottages. Many of these also had back-to-back cupboards with secret doors. Contraband could be shifted from shore to bank top without emerging into daylight.

The tunnel

An anti-smuggling squad of six Dragoons was billeted at 'Bay' in 1775, but smugglers often escaped along The Bolts, a narrow street leading to woodland. Some historians believe that when smuggling eventually faded of its own accord, it was the wealth derived from it that enabled Bay folk to invest in ships.

In the past two centuries 200 Bay cottages have fallen into the sea, slimming the village to half its former size. The losses include the top end of King Street, the original main road, which collapsed in 1780. From the Dock its rump now leads to the massive serpentine-shaped sea wall – the tallest in Britain at 40ft (12m), built in 1973–4.

Among buildings still facing the full force of the sea is the **Bay Hotel**. In 1843 it was almost destroyed, and in another storm the bowsprit of a sailing ship, wrecked against inn's walls, ended up through one of the windows. A shelter at the Dock is the former **lifeboat house**. After 101 years' service, entirely with oar-powered lifeboats, the Bay station closed in 1931. A plaque at Bank Top recalls a remarkable rescue of 1881. With conditions too bad for the local boat to be launched, the Whitby boat, hitched to horses, was hauled six miles over snowdrifts to save the crew of a brig that had foundered off the Bay.

Bodies were washed up so often in the bay that a mortuary was built. Identified by its engraved euphemistic name Coroner's Room, up in Fisherhead, this now houses a ★ **small museum** (June to September daily except Saturday, 1.30–4pm, but 11am–4pm in July and August).

The ★ **cliffs and shore** at Robin Hood's Bay are good for fossil hunting and exploring rock pools.

Exploring the rock pools

Ravenscar's remote headland

Resuming at the car park, the route heads in the Scarborough direction, initially on minor roads and then the A171. At the Falcon Inn, the road to Ravenscar is taken.

The prominent radio mast marks the end of the Lyke Wake Walk (*see page 40*). The wide road into **Ravenscar**, and others at right angles off it, recall the ill-fated scheme to create a resort on this unlikely clifftop. Put forward by businessmen (mainly from West Yorkshire) in 1895, its catalyst was the opening of the Whitby–Scarborough section of the coastal railway ten years earlier. But though a prospectus was drawn up, few buyers emerged for the 1,200 building plots, spread over 750 windswept, fog-prone acres. A mere handful of homes arose along the broad boulevards, where manhole covers and grates now peep through grass. Most evocative is Station Square, the intended hub of the new town. Alongside the bramble-covered platform of the long-gone railway station, its single row of buildings, one of them now a café, faces the otherwise empty quadrangle.

The Romans had a signal station at Ravenscar. Now in Whitby Museum, its inscribed foundation stone was unearthed when the ★ **Raven Hall Hotel** was built in 1774 as a country mansion for a Captain Child, of London. Its later ownership by a physician to 'mad' George III (1760–1820) has led to a claim that it was used as a retreat, suitably remote from London, for nursing George through outs of insanity. In 1845, the physician's son, a notorious gambler, lost the hall in a wager over two woodlice crossing a saucer. The new owner, William Hammond, built the little church and the now-ruined windmill. Fifty years later, his son sold out to the business consortium, whose first act was to convert the hall into a hotel.

By the coast path near Ravenscar are the remains of the ★★ **Old Peak Alum Works** (National Trust, open all times), active 1640–1862. The nearby cliffs are an open manual of the coastal geology. A guidebook to a 3-mile (4.8-km) trail is available at the **Information Centre**.

If returning to Whitby, the route may be varied by taking the first right turn beyond Hawsker, giving ★ **strong views** of Whitby Abbey.

Catering to the crowds in Scarborough

Alternatively, continue down the A171 for a visit to ★ **Scarborough**. This thriving resort offers visitors two bays, a busy harbour and a castle on the cliff top. The South Bay has a typically brash English seafront, but the areas around the Spa and the North Bay have a pleasantly contrasting calm. A walk along the bracing **Marine Drive** linking North with South Bay is particularly recommended, as is a visit to the **Sea Life Centre** in North Bay, where a huge variety of fish, including sharks, can be viewed through perspex underwater tunnels. Behind the sea front of South Bay and up the hill is a modern shopping centre and an abundance of cafés and entertainment. The town has an enviable theatrical reputation built around Alan Ayckbourn, the local-born playwright, who premiers all his plays at the **Stephen Joseph Theatre**. On Castle Road, near the harbour in South Bay, the **Millennium Centre** documents 1,000 years of local history dating back to the Vikings. At the parish church near the castle is the grave of Anne Brontë.

Millennium Museum

Marine Drive

Historic Landscape

Opposite: Rievaulx Abbey

Few parts of Britain more potently evoke the distant past than the North York Moors. The formative eras in Britain's history are everywhere evident in the landscape.

Early Man

On the high moors it is possible to get close to some of Britain's earliest people. A visit to one of the prominent Bronze Age howes, or burial mounds, is the most obvious means – but not necessarily the best. For still scattered on the moor tops are plentiful examples of the flint tools and weapons used by the region's prehistoric inhabitants. Most are overlooked, because while a tanged and barbed arrowhead of the late Bronze Age is easily identified – and therefore swiftly removed – cruder earlier versions go unrecognised, as do tools like animal-skin scrapers, needles, and the blades of tiny knives and saws. Yet these are arguably more precious than a perfectly-formed arrowhead – or even a bronze dagger. For they are the first man-made objects in the moors. It is always a thrill to pick one up knowing that the last person to handle it lived on the moors between 10,000 and 1,700 years before Christ lived. Still razor-sharp, they will serve as a penknife – perhaps to slice a lunchtime apple.

The tools of Early Man

61

More than 250 listed prehistoric sites dot the Moors. In 1937 on Loose Howe, just off the Rosedale Abbey to Castleton road, the archaeologist Frank Elgee uncovered a rare 'boat burial'. A body, probably that of a Bronze Age chief, had been placed in a high-prowed canoe, with a similar vessel as a cover and a third alongside. Together with the grave goods, including a skin cloak and a dagger, these relics are in the British Museum.

A field path above Sunny Bank Farm, near Hawnby, passes a howe that was re-used in the 7th century. Interred there was an obviously important young woman, perhaps the daughter of a Saxon earl. Her hair had been fastened with gold and silver pins, and around her waist was a garnet-studded leather girdle with gold clasp and rivets. By her head was a fine bronze bowl.

On Cow Ridge, between Hawnby and Osmotherley, primitive walls of a Bronze Age field system can still be traced, while on Danby High Moor, around 800 hummocks consist of stones that were probably raked up as the moor was cleared for primitive cultivation. Wherever one goes, or even looks, on the high moors, early man has been there.

The Christian heritage

The Romans made only a marginal impression on the moors, despite their road across Wheeldale and its associated training camp (*see Historical Highlights, page 10*).

Roman road across Wheeldale

Stained glass at Lastingham

Mount Grace Priory

But the impact of Christianity was vast. In 626, the year before he founded York Minster, King Edwin of Northumbria was saved from an assassin's dagger by his courtier Lilla, who took the fatal, poisoned blow himself. In gratitude, Edwin erected a massive cross (*see page 34*) on Fylingdales Moor. Still there, this is believed to be the oldest Christian monument in the North of England.

Soon, three pre-Conquest abbeys were founded. Although no visible trace survives of the most famous, St Hilda's Whitby Abbey, ancient stones in Hackness church recall its daughter abbey of 680–869. Lastingham, too, had a pioneering abbey, and though it fell to Danish raiders in the 9th century, an attempt was made to revive it two centuries later. The crypt of this later abbey, which was abandoned because of Viking raids, is an astonishing monument beneath the parish church. In his *Collins Guide to English Parish Churches*, John Betjeman describes it as 'one of the most moving places in England'.

The Lastingham monks shifted to York, where they founded St Mary's Abbey. But 25 post-conquest abbeys and nunneries ultimately appeared in and around the moors, with 14 active at the Dissolution. Their adherence to 'Christian' ideals is a matter for debate. The Cistercian Rievaulx Abbey never welcomed strangers and ruthlessly evicted tenants on gifted land. Fearing any challenge to its authority, Benedictine Whitby Abbey imposed virtual tyranny on the town, where locals even had to pay road tolls. The abbey's demise was the signal for Whitby's expansion, beginning with the building of its first piers. Meanwhile, the Byland Cistercians evicted an entire community to build their short-lived abbey near Rievaulx. And although that community was rehoused nearby, most of the 60 or so others ousted by the Cistercians in Yorkshire weren't so lucky.

Only the Carthusian monks at Mount Grace maintained their piety to the end, and they alone still enjoyed the respect of local people. But even they would be surprised that the major legacy of the abbeys is the landscape. They tamed the valleys and turned the high ground into sheep runs, setting the seal on the moors in their present form.

Crosses on the moors

An appealing minor legacy is a network of paved roads – like that linking Whitby Abbey with a priory at Grosmont, and another crossing Urra Moor, Bilsdale – part of Rievaulx Abbey's route to its fishery at Teesmouth. But more obviously part of the region's Christian heritage are its moorland crosses, of which more than 30 exist in part or whole. Unlike the very early Lilla Cross (*see above*), most were erected as medieval waymarkers, to give Christian comfort to those crossing the lonely wastes.

Young Ralph

On Cropton cross, whose stump is in the churchyard, a flagon of fresh water was kept for travellers. On certain other crosses, those who could afford it placed coins for more needy wayfarers. This custom endures, and in 1961, the shaft of the cross on Blakey Ridge – Young Ralph, the national park's emblem (*see page 23*) – snapped as a local man climbed to collect the coins.

63

It is said that if Young Ralph meets Fat Betty, a whitewashed cross-base along the nearby Rosedale road, there will be a wedding. A little less improbable, but illustrating the depth of the early Christian tradition, is a tale that Old Ralph, another neighbour of Young Ralph, marks where a Rosedale man of that name reunited the prioresses of Rosedale and Baysdale nunneries, who got lost in a storm while settling a boundary dispute. Ralph found Sister Betty where Fat Betty now stands and Sister Margery by an upright stone that has ever since borne her name.

The two Ralphs are so ingrained in local culture that there is a saying: Stiff as Ralph Cross.

Viking influence

The largest pre-Conquest colonisation of the moors, by the Vikings, has left a marked and enduring impression on local language. On maps, there are many topographical terms of Viking origin: *foss* marks a waterfall, *wath* a ford and *griff* a steep-sided valley. Every moorland farmer commonly uses the old Norse word *yan*, meaning *one*, and many say *shut yat* if they want you to close the gate: walkers please note. Some moorland folk still say *slape* instead of *slippy*, and to one and all the mole-catcher is *t' mowdy man* – *mowdy* being Norse for *mole*. There is also *beck* (originally *bek*) to refer to a stream; *roke* is a sea mist; and *rigg and furr* refers to the ridge-and-furrow profile of an old field. If a Viking turned up at a moorland sheep sale, he would feel quite at home.

The Vikings left their mark

Literature and Folklore

Literature

Sleeping with his animals one night, Caedmon, an illiterate cowherd at Whitby Abbey in the 7th century, dreamed that an angel appeared and invited him to 'sing of the beginning of things'. Initially reluctant, Caedmon did so. The next morning he repeated the song to the astonished monks, who wrote it down. His *Song of Creation* is regarded as the birth of English Literature, and Caedmon is honoured by a prominent cross in Whitby's clifftop St Mary's churchyard, where it was unveiled by the then Poet Laureate Alfred Austin in 1898.

Since Caedmon's time, other authors have been inspired by the North York Moors and their coast. Key episodes of *Dracula* are set in Whitby, where author Bram Stoker wrote chapters of his Gothic masterpiece. A Dracula Trail links the highlights.

Lewis Carroll

Lewis Carroll is believed to have derived the idea of *Through the Looking Glass*, sequel to *Alice in Wonderland*, from a large gilt mirror in lodgings at No 5, East Terrace, Whitby. His first published writings, a story and comic poems, appeared in the *Whitby Gazette* while he was staying in the town as a student in 1854.

William Wordsworth

A visit to Rievaulx Abbey with her brother William inspired a lovely passage in the *Journals of Dorothy Wordsworth*. And their most anguished entry relates to William's marriage to Mary Hutchinson at Brompton, near Scarborough, in 1802. Dorothy, who had an exceptionally close relationship with her brother, couldn't bear to witness the ceremony and remained in Mary's farmhouse. 'I could stand it no longer,' she writes. 'I threw myself on the bed, where I lay in stillness…'

Laurence Sterne

Earlier, in his vicarage at Coxwold, near Thirsk, Laurence Sterne (1713–68) penned his witty and irreverent books *Tristram Shandy* and *A Sentimental Journey*, which contributed greatly to the development of the novel.

Folklore and festivals

Tradition runs deep in the North York Moors. The region's former isolation remains mirrored in the vigour of old pastimes and often strange customs.

Down into the harbour mud at Whitby one morning each spring go three men, two of whom set about erecting a short fence of interwoven hazel stakes. As they complete their task, their companion blows a horn and bellows: 'Out on ye, out on ye, out on ye'. Known as the Penny Hedge ceremony, this almost certainly originates in some forgotten tithe of Whitby Abbey. However, legend has it that in 1159 three landowners out hunting a wild boar inflicted fatal wounds on a hermit monk who sheltered the animal. On his deathbed, the monk forgave his attackers in return for a penance. On pain of forfeiting their land, at 9am on Ascension Eve – 38 days after Easter Sunday – they and their successors were to plant a 'hedge' in the harbour that must withstand three tides. The stakes for the hedge were to be cut with a 'knife of one penny price.'

Equally mystifying to many visitors are prominent boxes on village greens in and around the Esk Valley. They protect the clay of quoits pitches. Teams play in an evening league, and on Saturday there are open championships. The tyro soon discovers that the greatest skill lies not in pitching the 5¼-lb (2.8-kg) iron quoit cleanly over the pin but preventing rivals reaching the target.

The Esk Valley also has a long-standing tradition of gooseberry growing. Founded in 1800, the **Egton Bridge Old Gooseberry Show** is now one of just two in Britain devoted to the humble goosegog. Specimens as big as golf balls are produced by methods varying from feeding with ankle deep manure to painstakingly tying cans of water below potential winning berries. With brass band, public tea and a solemn 'weigh-in', showday, the first Tuesday in August, is a delightful moorland occasion.

Shearing time

65

The 'feel' of moorland life today is perhaps obtained best at one of the **agricultural shows** still staged by most dales. Kildale also holds a **Mell Supper**. Traditionally this marked the bringing in of the last sheaf. In a hall decked like a church at harvest festival, each of Kildale's supper-goers is served a slice of the traditional Mell Cake, a kind of spicy teacake baked by local women.

Still observed at Goathland is **Plough Sunday** – the Sunday preceding the January Monday when ploughboys traditionally returned to the land. At Morning Service, a replica plough is carried to the chancel by the Goathland Plough Stots, Britain's longest-established team of long-sword dancers. Their name is an old word for a young bullock, and their dances were originally fertility rites.

Still sitting annually at Spaunton, near Hutton-le-Hole, and Danby, Eskdale, are two **Courts Leet** – traditional manor courts. Composed of locally elected jurymen, their task is to safeguard and administer the common rights and privileges on manor estates. Their main business is the annual collection of 'fines' – in reality small charges made for permitted encroachments, like a trestle tea-shop sign or a flagged path to a cottage. Any non-attending 'freeholder', a person with a right to run sheep or cut turf or peat, faces a real fine, at Danby 2p.

'Morning and Evening' by Whitby's Frank Sutcliffe

More Whitby tradition

Back at Whitby, each July brings another colourful harbourside ceremony, when the Bishop of Whitby **blesses the boats**. As ancient as the Penny Hedge? Not quite – it dates from 1948. However, only a place with lively old traditions creates new ones.

Tourists crossing the moors in late July and August often catch sight of bent figures among the heather. Local people and visitors from nearby towns are gathering the small purple fruits of the **bilberry**, a plant intimately associated with the heather. The reward for their backaching labour is a delicious pie, most delightfully served with ice cream. Though bilberry pie is now a rarity on moorland menus for visitors, the other great harvest of the moors, heather honey, remains widely available in shops and at beekeepers' garden gates. Darker and stronger-flavoured than flower honey, it is the product of bees whose hives have been put out on the moors when the heather is in bloom. With a beekeeper as guide, an exhibition of 'the living **honey bee**' can be seen at East Ayton, near Scarborough (daily 10am–5pm).

At Ampleforth, the moors steal a march on apparently more balmy areas. Ampleforth Abbey's 7-acre (3-hectare) commercial **apple orchard** is the most northerly in England and, at 650ft (200m), one of the highest in Britain. From August to April most of its 60 varieties, including rarities like Yorkshire Cockpit, are on sale at the orchard, which is open for group visits (tel: 01439 788485).

Licked with relish on even the coldest winter's day, Suggitt's **traditional ice cream** (*see page 43*) probably draws more visitors to Great Ayton than Captain Cook. Together with a Petch's pork pie, an equally prized local delicacy, a tub of Suggitt's was presented to the Archbishop of York on an official visit in 1996.

That Yorkshire tradition **high tea** – fish and chips or salad, followed by cakes and scones, washed down with lashings of tea – is an institution at Helmsley's Crown Hotel, where it is served in a cosy Jacobean dining room.

A wide range of **organically-produced food**, including bread, biscuits, jam, chutney and curds, are on sale at Botton Village (*see page 44*), while over at Cropton, near Pickering, the New Inn offers **prize-winning ales** from its own brewery, open to visitors.

At Whitby, **kippers** cured over oak chippings can be bought direct from Fortune's kipper house, whose aromatic smoke, drifting up the cliff from Henrietta Street, sometimes puzzles visitors to St Mary's church. Fortunes have been kippering herrings since 1872, and visitors may catch a glimpse of the fish being hung up or taken down among the incredibly tarred beams and rafters of the seemingly ramshackle kipper house.

Of course Whitby Crab is well signalled throughout the town. But equally prized as Whitby delicacies by those who know the town are various products of Botham's Bakery, especially lemon buns and butter buns, a super-creamy

Try some Suggitt's

67

Brooke Bond Tea is good tea

Freshly-smoked kippers

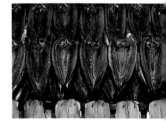

cream bun. Still in the family of Elizabeth Botham, who founded the bakery in 1865, this treasured local business now enterprisingly sells its wares on the Internet (http://goole.octacon.co.uk/ext/bothams). Botham's plum bread has gone to Peru.

Restaurants
In the following selection, **£££** = expensive (dinner with wine over £50 for two); **££** = moderate (£30–50); **£** = inexpensive (under £30).

Pickering
White Swan, Market Place, tel: 01751 472288. Prides itself on satisfying the healthy appetites of walkers ££. **The Lodge**, Middleton Road, tel: 01751 472976. Recently-opened bistro, sister to Chapters of Stokesley, which is listed by Egon Ronay, Which, and Michelin. International menu focused mainly on European dishes ££.

Sinnington, near Kirkbymoorside
Sinnington Country Hotel, tel: 01751 431577. Rich and inventive sources helped gain an AA food rosette for this local pub-turned country hotel, in a bypassed village with daffodil-adorned green and maypole ££.

Rosedale
Milburn Arms, Rosedale Abbey, tel: 01751 417321. Very appealing country hotel with high reputation for flair with British food. Two AA rosettes and Les Routiers ££.

The Milburn Arms

Blakey Ridge
The Lion, between Castleton and Hutton-le-Hole, tel: 01751 417320. Sound largely traditional fare keeps all-comers happy in this famous moortop pub, whose snug interior has open fires and breathtaking views ££.

Helmsley
The Crown Hotel

Crown Hotel, Market Square, tel: 01439 770297. Comfortable former posting house offering a wide choice of country-style cooking ££. **Feversham Arms**, High Street, 01439 770766. Well-varied table d'hote using top quality English food, including local game in season £££.

Coxwold
Fauconberg Arms, tel: 01347 868214. Historic 17th-century inn long renowned for good food ££.

Osmotherley
Three Tuns, tel: 01609 883301. Cosy village inn listed by Egon Ronay, AA, Camra, Les Routiers. English and French cuisine, with emphasis on fresh fish ££.

Great Broughton, near Stokesley
Jet Miners Inn, tel: 01642 712427. Much praised by Coast to Coast walkers, its dependable bar and a-la-carte food is served in either a conservatory or low-beamed bar with open fire, where jet jewellery makers from Whitby bartered prices with local jet miners ££.

The Fox and Hounds

Ainthorpe, near Danby, Eskdale
Fox and Hounds, tel: 01287 66021. Probably the biggest selection of vegetarian and vegan dishes in the moors, prepared by vegetarian co-proprietor who also provides mainstream meals £.

Goathland
Mallyan Spout, tel: 01947 896206. Traditional English food with fish bias is the speciality of this ivy-clad late Victorian hotel, holder of an AA food rosette ££.

Staithes
Endeavour Restaurant, tel: 01947 840825. Egon Ronay quayside restaurant serving chiefly imaginative dishes using local seafood – e.g. pan-fried codroe with Indian aubergine salads ££.

Queues at the Magpie

69

Whitby
The Magpie Café, Pier Road, tel: 01947 602058. Legendary harbourside restaurant in merchant's house that became the Pilotage. Though most famed for its superb Whitby fish and chips, it satisfies most other tastes with equal aplomb. Children's menu ££. **Royal Fisheries**, Baxtergate, tel: 01947 604738. Fish and chips to rival The Magpie in café adjoining takeaway £.

Moors Railway, tel: 01751 472508. Dine on the move. Five-course dinner in a Pullman, May to September Friday and Saturday evening, Sunday lunch April to October. Price includes fare £££.

Tearooms
Below are some tearooms offering good home-baked fare in attractive settings. The Singing Bird, **Kilburn**, has local watercolours for sale. Forge Tea Room, **Hutton-le-Hole**, serves local ice-cream. The flagged-floored Prudom House, **Goathland**, shows local crafts. The Stonehouse Bakery and the Tearoom, **Danby**, has jams for sale. Shepherd's Hall, **Lealholm**, also does farmhouse ham-and-eggs. **Coxwold** Tea Rooms is another stronghold of Yorkshire high tea. Chequers, near **Osmotherley**, also sells honey, game and mineral water from its own spring. Lord's Stone Café, **Carlton Bank**, near Stokesley, was built into the hillside in 1991 – a brilliant piece of design.

Cream tea at the Singing Bird

Sea canoeist

Active Holidays

There are many ways of actively enjoying the North York Moors. The best is undoubtedly on foot, for the national park's 1,100 miles (1,770km) of rights of way offer unmatched opportunities to experience the region's scenic variety and exhilarating sense of freedom.

Walking

Planning the next stage

The many walking guides from information centres and shops describe walks from easy strolls to the 42-mile (68-km) Lyke Wake Walk (*see page 40*) and the 108-mile (175-km) Cleveland Way, the long-distance trail from Helmsley to Filey around the spectacular edge of the national park.

A score of family walks are outlined in inexpensive leaflets by the national park authority (tel: 01439 770657). Two packs entitled Six of the Best describe circular walks based on the Cleveland Way, one inland, the other on the coast. A booklet on the 30-mile (50-km) Esk Valley Walk, following the river from source to Whitby, divides the route into easy day walks, using the scenic Esk Valley railway (Middlesborough–Whitby) for the return.

Forest Enterprise (tel: 01751 460295 or 472771) also has a series of waymarked walks. One, at Littlebeck, goes through deciduous woodland with an attractive waterfall and Hermitage folly – a cave hewn from a huge rock.

Cycling

Miles of quiet roads, bridleways and forest tracks are ideal for cycling. A 70-mile (110-km) network of Forest Enterprise cycle tracks caters for tourers and off-road specialists. The Forest Enterprise booklet *Pedal and Puff* links three routes of graded severity to the Moors Railway. Mountain bikes can be hired at a number of centres.

Horse-riding

The national park has many horse-riding centres, offering treks from an hour to a day. Locations include: Boltby, near Thirsk, tel: 01845 537392; Great Fryup, Eskdale, tel: 01947 897470; Irton, near Scarborough, tel: 01723 863466; Ingleby Greenhow, near Stokesley, tel: 01642 778331; Robin Hood's Bay, tel: 01947 880249; Sleights, near Whitby, tel: 01947 810415.

The longest forest horse trail is the 35-mile (56-km) Newtondale Trail. Based on Pickering, it embraces moor and farmland through Newton Dale (*see page 35*) to Grosmont and back via Goathland and Levisham. More novel is a two-day llama trek on the former Scarborough–Whitby railway (tel: 01842 878181).

Gliding

To glide the moors for 20 minutes, book at the Yorkshire Gliding Club, Sutton Bank (tel: 01845 597237), or Carlton Moor Gliding Club, by Stokesley (tel: 01642 778234).

Ready for take-off

Outward bound

Orienteering can be tried in Dalby Forest (maps at Visitor Centre), and half- or full-day instruction in canoeing, climbing and white-water rafting can be booked at: Ingleby Cross, near Osmotherley, tel: 01609 882571; Littlebeck, near Whitby, tel: 01947 810673; Cropton, tel: 01751 417228; and Staithes, tel: 01947 840757.

71

Sailing

Sailing dinghies can be hired at Wykeham Lake, near Scarborough, and sailing by permit is available weekdays on Scaling Dam Reservoir, between Whitby and Guisborough. Rowing boats can be hired at Ruswarp, on the Esk.

Fishing

River fishing is available on Dalby Beck (tickets from Dalby Forest Visitor Centre), the Derwent at Hackness (Hackness Grange Hotel), and the Esk at Danby (Duke of Wellington Inn) and Sleights (Mr Simms, tel: 01947 604658). Lake and reservoir fishing is at: Cod Beck Reservoir, Osmotherley; Larner Lake, Little Ayton; Scaling Dam and Lockwood Beck Reservoir; Low Osgoodby Lake, Sutton Bank, tel: 01845 597601; Moorland Trout Lake, Pickering, tel: 01751 474219; Hazel Head, Saltersgate, tel: 01751 460215; and Wykeham Lakes, tel: 01723 863148.

Starting young

Birdwatching

Most birdwatching in the national park is done on walks. Bird tables at a car park in Forge Valley (*see page 37*) attract woodland birds. Book early for Forest Enterprise walks to see and hear the nightjar (tel: 01751 472771).

Getting There

Opposite: making tracks

By plane

The North York Moors are within easy reach of the northern conurbations, which are served by the following airports: Manchester Airport, tel: 0161 489 3000. Leeds/Bradford Airport, tel: 0113 250 9696. Teesside Airport, tel: 01325 332 811. Newcastle Airport, tel: 0191 286 0966.

By ship

Hull is a popular port of arrival for visitors from the Continent. It is two hours drive from the national park, and there are bus and rail links to York and Scarborough.

By train

East Coast Main Line services between London and Edinburgh and Trans-Pennine services from Manchester and Liverpool stop at York, which has regular services to Thirsk and Northallerton. Regional Railways routes link York to Malton and Scarborough. Information from York Station, tel: 01904 642155. East Coast Main Line trains also stop at Darlington, which connects with Middlesbrough, where you can take the highly picturesque line to Whitby down the Esk Valley. This line links at Grosmont with steam trains from Pickering on the North Yorkshire Moors Railway.

By car

The main arteries serving the moors are the A1 and the A19. West of York, the A1 crosses the A64 from Leeds to Scarborough. From the A64, the A169 via Malton and Pickering leads to the eastern part of the national park, and the coast around Whitby. For Helmsley and the central moors, choose between the meandering B1393 from York, or the A170, which branches off the A19 at Thirsk and climbs Sutton Bank. The A19 runs close to the Hambleton Hills then crosses the A172, which runs north of the Cleveland Hills. From the North, the main access is either the A19, linking with the A174 Middlesbrough to Whitby road, or the A1, linking with the A170 at Thirsk.

By coach

National Express (tel: 0990 808080) services link York and Leeds with most other major towns. There is a National Express service from Hull to York. Yorkshire Coastliner (tel: 01653 692556) operates bus services along a number of routes to Pickering, Whitby and Scarborough. National Express buses to Darlington and Middlesbrough link with the trains of the Esk Valley Railway. Special services from Darlington, Hull, Beverley and Driffield connect with the Moorsbus service (*see page 74*).

It's quicker by rail

SCARBOROUGH
IT'S QUICKER BY RAIL

SLOW

Getting Around

By bus

The North York Moors national park authority operates Moorsbus – a network of buses on various routes around the moors. It runs every Sunday and Bank Holiday Monday from 26 May to 29 September, and every Tuesday and Wednesday from 23 July to 28 August. Moorsbus and Moors Connections timetables are available from tourist information centres and the national park centres, or tel: 0891 664342.

United and Tees operate services from Teesside to Whitby and Scarborough – both along the coast and across the moors – as well as local services around Stokesley, Thirsk, Northallerton and Osmotherley. For timetables write to: North East Bus Ltd, United House, Grange Road, Darlington DL1 5NL. SSB Coaches of Northallerton, tel: 01609 778132, operates a Friday service from Stokesley to Helmsley. A service between Thirsk and Malton by Slingsby-based Stephenson's also calls at Helmsley, tel: 01347 838990 or 821707.

Pickering station

By train

The North Yorkshire Moors Railway operates a daily steam service from April to the end of October. Contact the NYMR at Pickering Station, tel: 01751 472508. For details of the Middlesbrough to Whitby Esk Valley service, tel: 0191 232 6262.

By bike

The moors offer splendid cycling opportunities (*see page 70*). For bike-hire, including mountain bikes, contact the relevant Tourist Information Office (*see page 75*).

Travel for the disabled

A free booklet, *British Rail and Disabled Travellers*, outlines facilities and fare concessions for disabled rail travellers. To arrange assistance in advance, tel: 01904 653022, or 0113 2411692. Disabled people travelling by bus should contact the company. A county-wide guide for the disabled, *Out and About in Yorkshire & Humberside*, is available for a small charge from the regional tourist board, tel: 01904 707961. A 3½-mile (5.5-km) 'tactile trail' for the blind and partially sighted links Grosmont and Goathland. Contact the national park headquarters for details.

Maps

Numbers 26 and 27 of the Ordnance Survey's Outdoor Leisure Series cover the North York Moors, including the coast, at a scale of 4 centimeters to 1 kilometre (1:25,000). They are widely available.

Facts for the Visitor

Service with a smile

Tourist Information

A huge amount of information is available at National Park Centres and Tourist Information Centres (TICs).

North York Moors national park headquarters, The Old Vicarage, Bondgate, Helmsley, York YO6 5BP, tel: 01439 770657.

National Park Centres

The Moors Centre, Danby, York, YO21 2NB, tel: 01287 660654. Sutton Bank Visitor Centre, Thirsk, YO7 2EK, tel: 01845 597426.

TICs

Helmsley, Market Place, tel: 01439 770173; **Whitby**, Langbourne Road, tel: 01947 810473; **Scarborough**, Valley Bridge Parade, tel: 01723 37333; **Easingwold**, Chapel Lane, tel: 01347 821530; **Goathland**, Village Store, tel: 01947 896207; **Great Ayton**, High Green, tel: 01642 722835; **Guisborough**, Church Street, tel: 01287 633801; **Hutton-le-Hole**, Ryedale Folk Museum, tel: 01751 417367; **Northallerton**, Applegarth, tel: 01609 776864; **Pickering**, Eastgate, tel: 01751 473791; **Ravenscar**, National Trust Coastal Centre, tel: 01723 870138; **Dalby Forest Visitor Centre**, tel: 01751 460295.

Post Offices

In the market towns and villages, Post Offices are often in other shops. Ask locally. Opening times and services are usually displayed in the window, and collection times are printed on letter boxes.

Market Days

Monday: Pickering, Thirsk.
Wednesday: Kirkbymoorside, Northallerton.
Friday: Helmsley, Stokesley, Easingwold.

Guaranteed delivery

Medical Centres

Most towns have a health centre. For details contact TICs or the local library. The main hospitals for the area are at Scarborough, York, Northallerton and Middlesbrough.

Emergencies

Dial 999 and ask for the appropriate service.

Newspapers

Mouseman furniture

Two regional morning newspapers, *The Northern Echo*, published in Darlington, and the *Yorkshire Post*, published in Leeds, circulate strongly in the Moors. Between them, the *Yorkshire Evening Press*, published in York, and the *Evening Gazette*, in Middlesbrough, cover the entire area. The weekly *Malton Gazette and Herald*, published in York, covers most of the southern dales, while the *Whitby Gazette* serves Eskdale and most of the coast. The Darlington-based *Darlington and Stockton Times* covers the northern and western parts of the Moors.

Souvenirs and craft goods

The North York Moors are home to a large number of craft workshops. Best known is the 'Mouseman' furniture workshop at Kilburn (*see page 17*).

Furniture: Eric & Stuart Gott, Priestley Butts, Whitby Road, Pickering, tel: 01751 472009 – period furniture of supreme quality, chiefly Georgian but also Tudor. Old Mill Furniture, Balk, near Thirsk, tel: 01845 597227 – traditional and modern in ten 'showroom' styles or to order. Treske, Thirsk, tel: 01845 522770 – domestic furniture produced in large workshop with visitor centre and café.

Traditional glass

Pottery and glassware: Wold Pottery, Harome, near Helmsley, tel: 01439 770927. Bob Bruce, 13 Park Terrace, Whitby, tel: 01947 600513 – stained-glass windows. Philip Chan and Cathy Abbott, Betton Farm, East Ayton, tel: 01723 865100 – Japanese techniques used to make pottery shown in the Victoria and Albert Museum. Rosedale Glass Gallery, Rosedale Abbey, tel: 01751 417550 – glass-making using traditional blowing techniques.

More craftworkers are listed in a booklet entitled *Brigantia*, available at TICs.

Galleries

Montage Studio, Castleton, tel: 01287 660159 – paintings, pottery and jewellery. Look Gallery, Castlegate, Helmsley, tel: 01439 770545 – good-quality paintings, traditional and modern. William Sissons, Market Place, Helmsley, tel: 01439 771385 – sporting pictures. Country Gallery, High Street, Great Ayton, tel: 01642 723976 – local watercolours. Abbey Galleries (John Freeman), Market Place, Whitby, tel: 01947 602799 – watercolours and prints.

The Moors for Children

There are many safe yet exciting places for children in the North York Moors. Popular **picnic spots** by moorland streams include Sheepwash near Osmotherley, Hob Hole in Westerdale and May Beck near Littlebeck. Along the coast, Sandsend, Whitby and Runswick Bay have particularly **fine beaches**, while for young explorers Staithes and the broad expanses of Robin Hood's Bay are noted for their rock pools.

Fun in Dalby Forest

Besides its famous 199 steps and walk-through whale's jawbone, Whitby has much to interest, and excite, the young. From the large fossils of prehistoric reptiles to a set of Eskimo false teeth carved from walrus tusks, a veritable treasure trove of fascinating exhibits await young and old in **Whitby Museum**, in Pannet Park. The rolling deck of a sailing ship is simulated in the **Museum of Victorian Whitby**, Sandgate, while the **Dracula Experience**, on Marine Parade, presents the horror story with animation and special effects – for 'mature' children, perhaps.

The North York Moors national park organises many events for children and family groups. Mainly at the Moors Centre, Danby, these include kite flying and how to survive in the wild. It also has guided trails for children, rides with a park ranger, and adventure days at Sutton Bank. Details from the centres or national park headquarters. A 'habitat trail' and orienteering are features of a similar programme based on Dalby Forest, tel: 01751 473810, while the National Trust conducts guided walks for children around the Bridestones, the fascinatingly-shaped rock outcrops near the forest, tel: 01751 460369.

77

Demonstrations of working heavy horses are given at the **Staintondale Shire Horse Farm**, near Ravenscar, tel: 01287 642877, and the life of the honey bee is imaginatively presented at the East Ayton **Honey Farm** (*see pages 37 and 67*). There are frequent open days at **Sour Leys** farm, near Helmsley, which has sheep, cows and a Clydesdale horse, giving an insight into a working farm. With more than 500 rabbits and guinea pigs, plus pot bellied pigs, sheep and goats, **Bunnyland** will delight most toddlers and young children. It sits on the edge of the moors between Whitby and Guisborough.

Family outing to Mount Grace

Three attractions worth mentioning lie just outside the national park near Malton: **Flamingo Land**, the North's biggest theme park and zoo; **Eden Camp**, an acclaimed World War II 'theme' museum; and Eden Farm, another working farm. Scarborough, too, has much to please children, perhaps on a day set aside from exploring the moors. In addition to its beaches, Scarborough attractions include the play park **Kinderland**, the fascinating **Sea Life Centre**, and boating on the excellent Peasholm Park lake.

A satisfied customer

Accommodation

Accommodation in the North York Moors ranges from basic-but-clean all the way to luxury hotels. B&Bs and guest houses cost £12–25 a night, hotels £15–90. Inns also offer accommodation for £14–28 a night. TICs hold accommodation registers and will usually help with booking.

Rented self-catering apartments, farmhouses and country cottages are available. Typical prices are around £100 a week in the low season to over £400 in the peak season. For details, try Moorland Holiday Cottages, Byre Cottage, Hutton-le-Hole, tel: 01751 417743.

Hotel and farm selection
Below is a short selection of comfortable accommodation for bed and breakfast or longer stays. **£** = up to £29 a night; **££** = £30–59; **£££** = £60 and over.

Castleton
The Moorlands Hotel, High Street, tel: 01287 660206. Wonderful position with views of the Esk Valley and Danby Dale £.

Farndale
Hollins Lodge, tel: 01751 433436. Former shooting lodge in beautiful gardens with marvellous views £.

Glaisdale
Egton Banks Farm, tel: 01947 897242. 18th-century farmhouse on beautifully situated working farm. Friendly, comfortable atmosphere £.

Goathland
Dale End Farm, Green End, tel: 01947 895371. In what is known as 'Heartbeat Country,' 500-year-old working farm whose livestock includes llamas £.

Great Broughton
Shirley Mead, Hilton House, tel: 01642 712526. Comfortable accommodation in former village bakehouse £.

Helmsley
The Black Swan Hotel, Market Place, tel: 01439 770466. Extremely comfortable Forte Heritage hotel overlooking the market place £££. **Stilworth House**, 1 Church Street, tel: 01439 771072. Relaxed atmosphere in elegant Georgian town house near market square £.

Hutton-le-Hole
The Barn Hotel, tel: 01751 417311. Converted barn in one of the most picturesque moorland villages £.

The Black Swan

Ingleby Greenhow, Great Ayton
Manor House Farm, tel: 01642 722384. Cosy 16th-century farmhouse in secluded location of 164 acres of park and woodlands below the Cleveland Hills ££.

Kirkbymoorside
The George and Dragon Hotel, Market Place, tel: 01751 433334. Characterful 13th-century hotel ££.

Lastingham
The Blacksmiths' Arms, tel: 01751 417247. Charming village inn doubling as a Post Office, opposite the church with its famous crypt £.

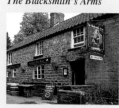

The Blacksmith's Arms

Osmotherley
The Queen Catherine Hotel, West End, tel: 01609 883-209. Family-run Grade II listed inn in pretty village £.

Pickering
Forest & Vale Hotel, Malton Road, tel: 01751 472722. Well-appointed Georgian manor house with attractive walled garden. Fine cuisine ££. **Bramwood Guest House**, Hallgarth, tel: 01751 474066. Snug 18th-century house, English cooking and no smoking £.

Robin Hood's Bay
Victoria Hotel, Station Road, tel: 01947 880205. Family-run hotel overlooking the bay £. **Rounton House**, Mount Pleasant South, tel: 01947 880341. Victorian House with garden and summer house £.

Rosedale Abbey
White Horse Farm Hotel, tel: 01751 417239. Comfortable and friendly Georgian inn with spectacular views ££. **Moordale House**, tel: 01751 417219. Fine Victorian house in own grounds amid beautiful moorland scenery £.

Runswick Bay
Cliffemount Hotel, tel: 01947 840103. Panoramic view over the bay £.

Staithes
Harbour Side Guest House, Seaton Garth, tel: 01947 841296. Grade II listed building overlooking harbour £.

Whitby
Saxonville Hotel, Ladysmith Avenue, tel: 01947 602631. Family-run hotel long in same ownership. Quiet location yet near shops and seafront £. **Wentworth House**, 27 Hudson Street, tel: 01947 602433. Comfortable accommodation in spacious Victorian house £.

Index